Rock Painting for Beginners

Learn How to Paint Rocks with 20 Easy Rock Painting Designs and Rock Painting Ideas with Pictures Included | Rock Painting Book for Kids and Adults

By

Angelica Lipsey

Disclaimer

This publication is designed to provide competent and reliable information regarding the subject matter covered. However, the views expressed in this publication are those of the author alone, and should not be taken as expert instruction or professional advice. The reader is responsible for his or her own actions.

The author hereby disclaims any responsibility or liability whatsoever that is incurred from the use or application of the contents of this publication by the purchaser or reader. The purchaser or reader is hereby responsible for his or her own actions.

Table of Contents

Introduction

In one way or the other, you might have come across a painted rock in your close surrounding or the art store. Either way, you may have also gazed and wondered how someone could create a masterpiece using a stone.

If you are searching for a cheap way to engage in creative art for yourself, your friends, or your family members, you may want to look into rock painting.

The art of painting rocks is soothing and comforting, and it is a perfect way to learn how to paint without really understanding how it works. Compared to the difficulties experienced in creating artistic images on boards, rock painting is pretty much more effortless.

In rock painting, the rock already has a measurement and shape. All you need do is to gather your paints and color, something that is worthwhile. Locating good stones is the only challenging aspect of rock painting, but asides from that, the process is smooth and can be completed within minutes.

This book sets out virtually all you need to get and do to paint your first rock, such as the tools and supplies needed, tips and techniques to help you in your first and subsequent projects, including rock painting ideas you can start right away, and so much more!

So, are you ready to begin? Then, let's get right into the art of rock painting.

Chapter 1

What is Rock Painting?

Rock painting is the art of decorating stones, pebbles, and rocks with pens, paints, or other designing items. In most instances, rock painting comes with an inspirational or educative message.

Painted rocks can also be in any shape or size, depending on what you want. The purpose of painting rock is to beautify your environment, spread love, and positivity to those around you.

Learning the process of painting rocks is simple, and only a committed individual can do it. The interesting thing about rock painting is that you don't have to break the bank to purchase the needed materials.

Fortunately, most rocks are free, so you only need to find one close to you, get the required painting materials, and begin to create amazing arts.

History of Rock Painting

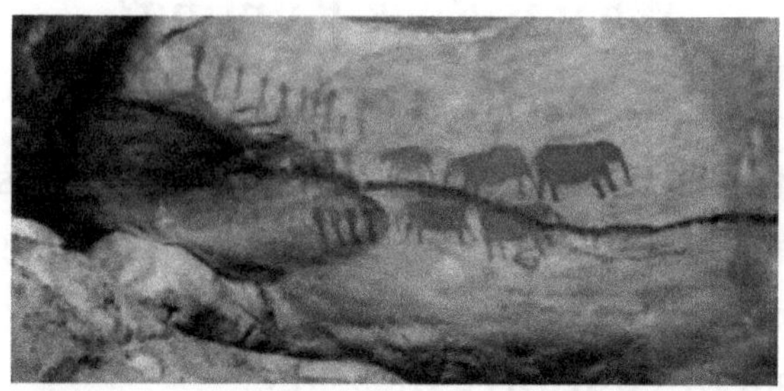

Rock painting is the earliest form of human-like creativity. Its first forms can be dated back to prehistoric times, up to 40,000 years ago.

In archaeology, rock art or rock painting is seen as human-made designs or messages designed on natural stone.

Generally, rock painting can be found in many continents worldwide, including Africa, Europe, South-East Asia, and Australia. The art of painting rocks also portrays religion, myths, rituals, legends, rivers, and mountains while sending important messages to all works of life.

In the earliest upper Paleolithic time, there was something referred to as pictographs paints. These paints were created with natural minerals and liquid, including urine, water, egg yolk, or blood. During that period, the artists would use a handmade brush, stamps, or their fingers to create the art.

Meanwhile, in today's world, rock painting is a method to express creativity. The amazing aspect of painting rocks is that it offers the artist a secure spot to create art without feeling thunderstruck in a large area.

How Does Rock Painting Work?

Rock painting works by decorating rocks with different designs and colors that suit the style you want. However, these rocks do not paint themselves; people take up these rocks and paint them to their satisfaction.

Meanwhile, do not fret because the process of rock painting is easy and straightforward. In addition, you don't need to spend too much to purchase the different materials needed to decorate a rock.

Anyone can do rock painting. You don't need to have all the required skills or be a talented artist to paint rocks. The only thing you need to have to paint rocks successfully is the desire and commitment to pick up a brush and learn. Learning the nitty-gritty of painting skills will take some time and consistent practice.

Undoubtedly speaking, children's art is the simplest form of painting rocks. On the other hand, other forms of painting rocks are also comfortable, but it requires intense dedication.

Now, let us discuss how rock painting works and how you can successfully create a beautiful rock by painting.

Getting rocks

Firstly, the most important material you will need before painting rocks is the rock itself. Without a rock, the term "rock painting" cannot work. So, how do you get rocks to beautify?

Well, rocks can be gotten almost everywhere you may find yourself in. Most people prefer to go outside their homes and pick rocks. If you stay in a place where hard stones are, it would be easy to spot a good rock for painting.

Alternatively, you can also go to the nearest park and pick any good rock you like. One important note here is that while selecting rocks, ensure you choose the one you know will fit perfectly with what you want for your design.

You shouldn't take any rock just because you are convinced it is a rock. The selected rock must be able to serve its purpose and suit your style. You wouldn't like to get home to discover that you picked the wrong rock and it won't fit in with what you want.

Other places where you can find rocks to use for your rock painting could be crafts or art stores. The beauty about buying rocks from an art store is that you have the opportunity to carefully select the one you want, depending on its looks, shape, or size.

While buying rocks from art stores or any landscaping business, endeavor not to purchase the ones that have a waxy film. This is because they will be much difficult to decorate with paint.

Materials needed to paint rocks

Below is the list of materials you will need to paint rocks:

- Acrylic paint
- Sealer
- Smooth rocks/stones
- Acrylic paint pens
- Sponge brushes

Preparation for rock painting

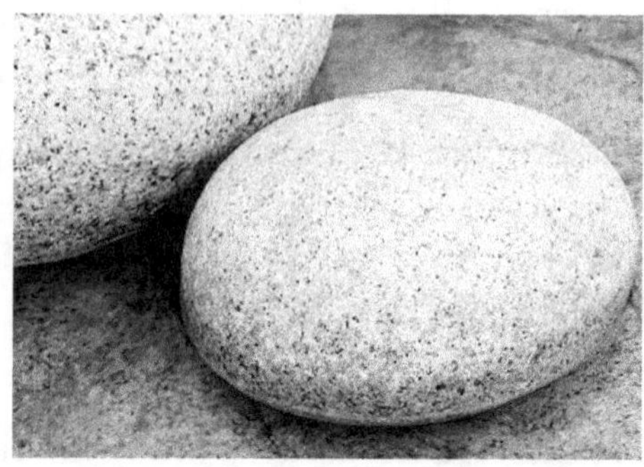

It would help if you prepared your rocks before painting them. One way to prepare for rock painting is to thoroughly wash your rocks and remove all dirt, sands, or seaweed.

Many people may ask if a base coat is needed before painting and decorating rocks. The use of a base coat is solely down to the artist and is not compulsory to use.

What's more, while preparing for rock painting, try and prime the rocks in a base coat of acrylic before you begin painting. Meanwhile, priming rocks are very common with people who use dark rocks or less rough rocks as the base coat to create an improved surface to draw or paint.

Selecting your best design

Before proceeding to begin painting your rocks, you need to choose your best design. Luckily, there are tons of trending designs worldwide that represent one thing or the other.

Depending on the reason for the rock painting, you may choose to paint a rock to send a peaceful message. The painting would then be done with peaceful colors like white.

It would help if you also looked into some rock painting design techniques like funny faces, landscapes, mandalas, and hand lettering. Nearly all the available designs involve mixing colors with acrylic paints or acrylic paint pens.

How can I make a painted rock?

If you need to know how rock painting works and how to create one, you should check the steps below:

Step 1: Locate or buy your favorite rock that will suit your design style. Ensure the rock you find or buy is flat and smooth because it would be much easier to paint.

Step 2: Clean your rock thoroughly with soap and clean water. While cleaning the rock, ensure you wipe out all dirt, sand, or weed that may be on the rock. Instead of using a hard brush or rigid cleaning equipment to clean your rock, opt to use a soft brush. Once you are done cleaning your rock, position it under the sun and leave it to dry.

Step 3: If you are convinced the rock is dry, proceed to take up your acrylic paint and paint the top part. Since you are painting your desired design, choose any paint you deem fit. After painting the top, leave the paint to dry on the rock.

Step 4: Once the rock's base coat has dried, you can add a fun design or write an inspirational quote like, "Hard work pays" on the rock. There are many inspirational or positive quotes you can pick and write on the rock.

The quote written on the rock should be done using an acrylic paint pen or any reliable paintbrush.

Step 5: Be patient and leave the design you have created to dry. To get the best result, you are advised to leave the painted design rock to dry all through the night.

Step 6: When the paint and paint pen has dried, you should then seal the rock with a sealer to protect and preserve the design.

Step 7: Leave the sealer to take effect, and you can begin to use the painted rock to create positivity around you.

If you made an error while painting your rock, you should paint on the entire rock's body and start the rock painting process once again. Do not forget that you cannot make a right or wrong step when painting rocks.

The painted rock's purpose is to spread love, share important messages, and bring smiles to people around you.

What to Do with Painted Rocks?

Painting rocks can be quite fun; however, you need to know what you will do with your already painted rock.

Different people have their specific reasons for painting rocks. While some people may prefer to spend their free time painting rocks, others like to present them as gifts or decorate their homes.

Here are some additional ideas that will aid you with what you should do with painted rocks.

- **Present them as gifts**

Are any of your close friends celebrating their birthday, or is there anyone celebrating close to you? Painted rocks can be presented as a birthday gift or for any celebratory reason.

All you need to do is find a rock, paint it to your taste, package it, and present it to the celebrant. You will be shocked to see that the painted rock gift will receive massive thanks and appreciation.

Many people do not know the value of rich painted rocks, and so they often ignore presenting them as gifts. On the other hand, those who know the value of painted rocks will receive the gift with a hand full of appreciation.

- **Donate them to hospitals**

Unless the hospital doesn't like good things, they might not accept your beautifully painted rock. As we all know, rocks are a perfect representation of our emotions, and their beautiful state could bring good luck to sick patients.

There is absolutely no reason why hospitals should reject your painted rocks. Even if they don't use them, they will most certainly keep them where it will be available for other people to see.

It may even interest you to know that some people might visit a particular hospital because they want to get a glimpse of a painted rock on display. If you have painted a rock and don't know what to do with it, you can donate them to hospitals.

- **Join a rock project like "The Kindness Rocks Project"**

There are tons of rock programs like "The Kindness Rock Project" that offers the chance for rock painters like you to showcase their rock painting skills alongside touching messages.

Since painted rocks tell a lot about certain situations, you can join similar projects and write encouraging messages for others to see.

For example, before joining The Kindness Rock Project, you will have to do the following:

a. Gather some rocks.
b. Carefully design or paint the rocks with non-harmful paint.
c. Use paint pens to create well-crated paint artwork.

d. Lastly, enhance your rock paint artwork with a non-harmful clear sealant.

- **Decorate your home or office**

Painted rocks can be used to decorate one's home or office. As an artist, you can easily paint a rock and place it in one corner of your home or office.

Aside from beautifying your home or office, it will also send a message to anyone who sees it that you love rocks. Additionally, people will see that you love good and beautiful things.

However, while decorating your home or office with beautifully painted rocks, ensure you don't turn into a rock hoarder. A rock hoarder is someone who gathers or accumulates plenty of rocks and positions them in one particular place.

Even if the rocks are beautiful, it still wouldn't be nice for people to see several painted rocks in your home or office. In fact, to some people, the high amount of painted rocks might infuriate them into questioning you rather than praising you.

- **Join a local rock group**

Joining a local rock group sounds pretty much interesting, and it also gives you the license to hoard rocks. In a rock group, their aims and objectives are to gather stones (painted or not), show their group members, and plan what to do with the rocks.

To discover a rock group close to you, search your town or city with the word "rocks" on Instagram or Facebook. Once you find a rock group near you, connect with them, and begin to rub minds with other rock lovers.

There is always a sense of excitement, knowing that you have something in common with a group of people. The group members are rock lovers like you, and they will do everything possible to amass more beautiful painted rocks for you.

- **Sell them**

Are you aware that beautifully painted rocks can earn you some cool cash? Well, now, you know. Some rock lovers who do not have the chance to paint rocks or gather rocks for painting will always prefer to pay people to receive painted rocks.

Your business is not what they are using the painted rock for but the money. Simply paint a rock, go to the artist market and sell your painted rock to a prospective buyer looking to pay big for it.

It will surprise you to know that painted rocks attracts a high amount, just like you have with painted drawings and others. One thing to take notice of is that an art lover will always purchase a painted rock for one reason or the other.

- **Assemble them**

Yes, you can paint rocks and assemble them anywhere you like. This may seem awkward, but it is an excellent way to begin your rock journey. If other artists see that you are a rock lover, they will like to associate with you, thereby connecting you with other rock lovers.

Since you are assembling your painted rocks, you can always take one out, especially when it represents that particular event. For example, there may be a specific painted rock meant for the beach. If you are going to the beach, you will have to take that particular painted rock along with you.

- **Auction for charity**

If you love donating to charity, you can auction your painted rocks and give the proceeds or some percentage to charity. This might seem a herculean task, but it is a good way for you to give to charity and serve the society in your own way.

Without a doubt, people will like to buy your painted rocks for a huge amount of money, especially knowing that you will give out the proceeds to charity.

- **Perform rock giveaway**

After painting several rocks and you don't want to keep or sell them, you can decide to perform giveaways to other rock lovers. While planning the giveaway exercise, ensure you make it as transparent as possible.

Furthermore, rock giveaways can also be done at Christmas or at any celebratory event where rock lovers are present. You will have a soft spot in people's hearts when you give them beautifully painted rocks for free.

Benefits of Rock Painting

Rock painting helps in improving the overall well-being of people, including their mental and physical health. It develops one's intellectual and emotional abilities for everyday activities.

As we all know, life is a challenging journey, and to move forward in life, we need to develop or set our minds in the right direction. Rock painting is one way to develop our mindset, improve our skills, and develop our sense of reasoning.

Age doesn't matter because rock painting is beneficial to both the old and the young. See below for the amazing health benefits of rock painting in the world we live in today:

Boosts memory

One of the health benefits of engaging in rock painting is to boost or develop our memory recollection abilities. Sadly, as we age, some diseases may spring up, which may slowly reduce our ability to remember certain things.

However, rock painting can help improve our minds by conceptual practice and imagining. Using our minds for actions such as painting helps in reducing the likelihood of emerging memory loss.

So, don't be surprised to notice a positive change in your ability to recall certain things when you begin painting rocks.

Relieves stress

Stress is undoubtedly a condition that everyone will experience at one stage in life. While experiencing stress may be good at certain times, a high level of stress can prove toxic to our health, both physically and mentally.

Rock painting can help ease stress and make one feel relaxed. As we paint, our minds become peaceful, thereby letting go of all current issues that pile up to cause stress and fear.

Consequently, when one is free from stress, their health and overall well-being will become a positive one to behold.

Improves communication skills

You may ask how does rock painting aid in the development of communication. Meanwhile, the truth remains that rock painting enhances communication skills with other individuals through art.

Since art involves expression, painting can offer assistance in expressing emotions and feelings without uttering any word. Furthermore, rock painting can also help individuals struggling with autism, shyness, and other social frailties.

Makes us happy

As we paint, we design beauty through artwork, thereby making us positive and happy towards life. You would never find any negativity in art.

Art is a perfect representation of happiness and positivity. When one decides to paint, the aim is to complete the project with a positive smile and a happy reaction.

Despite the challenges we experience, painting rocks enables us to be joyful through life. In fact, it boosts our self-esteem and encourages us to attain greater heights in our skill level and overall well-being.

It increases one's thinking ability

Most young folks prefer not to explore the art world and other things to expand their thinking ability. For some, painting is a natural way to enhance their creative skills and expand their imagination.

Imagine being able to think large and explore more? Isn't the feeling great? With rock painting, you can easily improve your imagination, which helps in brain development.

Enhances critical thinking

As we all know, rock painting enhances our creative skills. On the other hand, most individuals are not aware that it also enhances critical thinking.

When an artist starts to paint, some issues may likely come up, like the choice of color, where to paint, and so on. This is where our problem-solving skills come into play.

With rock painting, we can think outside the box and develop working solutions that will produce better results.

It heals us emotionally

Like mentioned earlier, painting allows us to express our emotions. Furthermore, the practice of painting inspires us to look inwards into our emotional state rather than our physical state.

Releasing emotions through rock painting can energize, revitalize, and restore our mental health, which may be rocked by some life challenges.

The form of emotional healing created by painting is often referred to as an abstract emotional expression. Several individuals who frequently paint have experienced high emotional healing and growth.

More often than not, a rock painter is often viewed by the state of work produced. This means that if a painting work portrays a sad picture, it means the painter is unhappy. However, if a painting is extremely beautiful and well crafted, the painter is likely in a happy state of mind.

Enhances fine motor skills

Generally, art has the potential to promote and enhance people's motion. The regular usage of gentle swish and paintbrushes of the hand encourages flexibility and motion in fingers and the hand as a whole.

Eye and hand management are important when painting rocks. While painting, our brains send signals to the motor neurons for directions on the next set of actions to take and how to carry out a task.

As a result, our motor skills are affected positively, which enables us to focus on any task, such as driving and examination.

Improves observation levels

Rock painting also allows us to become keen observers in different activities concerning life. Observation is a critical skill that allows us to notice the little things that happen around us.

Artists who have some years of experience in rock painting can attest that they have become keen observers wherever they may be. While painting rocks, details such as textures, shading, colors, and so much more are difficult to observe.

However, with consistent rock painting practice, you will closely observe them, improving your concentration and observation levels.

Chapter 2

Tips, Tricks, and Techniques of Rock Painting

Rock painting tips and tricks for beginners

Do you know you can become a professional rock painter without prior experience? Well, everything is achievable if you learn the method of painting rocks.

Remember that all professionals in the rock painting field didn't just become professionals. They went through a time-consuming process that converted them from beginners to professionals.

One exciting thing about becoming a professional in rock painting is that the criteria for becoming one are not dependent on your age, educational background, or experience in life.

It all boils down to learning the tips first before learning the techniques associated with painting rocks. Here, we have compiled several tips, and tricks beginners can follow to become rock painting professionals. They include:

1. **Learning the fundamentals of painting and drawing**

Learning the fundamentals of painting and drawing is the first and most crucial step in becoming a rock painting expert. You need to know everything about painting ground rules, like paint colors, designing, and others, to help you build your rock painting knowledge.

Without having any understanding of painting and drawing, you cannot become a professional rock painter.

2. **Finding a mentor**

Another important tip that will help you on your journey to becoming a professional rock painter is to find a mentor. A mentor can either be a popular person or even your close friend.

The most vital point to take here is to find someone you can look up to. Meanwhile, while looking up to someone, ensure you don't copy their rock painting style. Instead, trust your style and produce great results.

You can study your mentor's painted work and see how you can better the result without copying or comparing yourself.

3. Accepting criticism without complaining

Criticisms are normal when starting with just about anything. Instead of complaining bitterly about how others refused to acknowledge your painted work, build on their criticisms, and produce better work next time.

On the other hand, if the criticisms were stated to mock you, ensure you don't look in that direction because it could pull you down emotionally and mentally.

It would be best if you only accepted criticisms that are merited and constructive.

4. Continuing painting

When painting rocks as a beginner, you will surely make mistakes that may be laughable. However, since you are just starting your career as a rock painter, you should continue practicing painting until you become a professional.

Learning never stops, and you will continue to learn from your mistakes while painting rocks as a beginner.

5. Painting your imagination

As a beginner, you should inculcate the habit of abstractly painting rocks. In this age and time, abstract painting is rare because everyone wants to paint what they can see.

But if you want to build yourself, you need to paint what comes to your mind. This will massively help your creativity levels, especially when you become a professional.

6. Connecting with your fellow rock painters

Asides from having a mentor, you also need to connect with your fellow rock painters. For example, you can register in a local rock group and associate with your fellow rock painting colleagues.

They will even be willing to help you build your creativity and make you become a professional in a short period.

7. Don't procrastinate

Procrastination kills time and makes you lazy. If you want to become a professional rock painter, you must not procrastinate when painting rocks.

It is better to paint whenever you have the opportunity to rather than leaving it for a time you think is better. The sad thing about procrastination is that you may not even do it when you said you would.

8. Reading books related to rock painting

If you want to build your knowledge about rock painting, you should read many books related to rock painting.

Luckily, tons of books (both online and offline) are associated with rock painting that you can buy and begin reading.

Reading rock painting books will widen your horizon and make you more exposed to the world of painting rocks. You would even get to see more techniques and ideas that will make your rock painting work amazing.

9. Sleeping well

Since painting involves mental action, you should ensure you get enough sleep. If your mental health is operating below the optimal level, you will find it difficult to create stunning painted rocks.

Sleep is crucial in refreshing your mental health and enabling you to become more creative.

10. Be real

Tell yourself the truth when starting your rock painting journey. It won't do you any good if you are not honest with your rock painting outcome.

In fact, not being honest with yourself will make you feel good while actually, you are struggling to create well-painted rocks.

11. Exploring the art world

An artworld is a large place that needs to be explored if you want to know more about creating fine paint rocks. You can visit art places and try to discover the things that make a painted rock exceptional.

Additionally, you can enroll in a rock painting class and undergo training to sharpen your skills to make better-painted rocks.

Other rock painting tips and tricks that will help you attain success include:

1. Selecting a smooth and flat rock for painting

To achieve a successful rock painting result, you should select a smooth and flat rock. Bumpy and rough rocks can be used to paint, but it will be much harder and difficult to achieve the best result.

If you cannot see a smooth or flat rock around your area, you can visit the craft stores and purchase one for your rock painting exercise.

2. Thoroughly wash your rocks before painting

You wouldn't want to paint rocks when there are too much dirt and filth. Before painting your rock, you should ensure you remove all the filth and dirt so that it does not meddle with your design and spoil it.

A bar of dish soap should work just fine when used to wash your selected or purchased rock. Once done washing your rock, place it in an open area to dry.

3. Cover or seal the rock after painting

This is one important tip that, if not followed, can destroy all the work you have put into creating a beautiful design rock. You can use a spray sealer or brush to seal your rock.

Sealing your rock is essential as it prevents water and other harmful substances from messing up your rock. Prime white paint is another option to consider if you want to preserve your painted rock's bright color.

4. Paint your rock over and use many coats

Allow the paint to dry between the layers before using many coats to cover it. You can also use multi-surface or outdoor paint to offer assistance to your design.

5. Use smaller brushes

Ensure you use smaller brushes to create small dots or details. Alternatively, you can also use a stylus to create the same thing.

6. Use oil paint pens

You can use sharpies and oil paint pens to write an inspirational or educative message on your rock.

If you have any other option besides oil paint pens, you can use them to write an educative or motivational message on your rock. However, ensure you allow the paint to dry on the rock before writing anything.

7. Close your rocks using a coat

Depending on the rock type, you may choose to use two or more coats to close your painted rock.

These coats work best to preserve your beautiful design from harmful elements.

8. Erase everything if you make a mistake

Were you unfortunate enough to make a slight mistake? If that is the case, one important tip to follow is to wash off everything immediately when the paint is yet to dry.

Once the paint dries, it would be difficult or rather impossible to wash it off. To wash away the paint, dip an edge of a paper towel in water and wash off your rock.

Rock Painting Techniques

During your rock painting journey, you can embed different skills and techniques into your painting style to produce amazing results.

Furthermore, these techniques are for beginners who have little or no experience with painting rocks. Professionals are also not left out because the rock painting techniques listed in this chapter will help them achieve great outcomes.

If you are looking to discover new and unique rock painting techniques, the techniques below have you covered.

1. Simple Tracing Technique

Beginners mostly use the simple tracing technique to paint rocks at the initial stage. Usually, freehand painting can be a daunting task for starters; hence, the need to embed a simple or easy tracing technique.

The tracing technique is done by using a graphite transfer paper and a pencil. Here's what you have to do: Look for a design you want to paint on a rock and trace the pictorial design on the tracing paper. You can also print out a special design you want to trace.

The next step is to position the transfer paper on the rock you want to paint. Then the pictorial design or image should also be placed on top of the graphite transfer paper.

Without hesitation, take your pencil and trace the sketch of the design right before you. While tracing out the design, ensure you apply sufficient pressure. This will make the tracing line show clearly on the rock's body.

2. Blocking In

"Blocking In" is another popular rock painting technique that is used after sketching. Most people usually use the Blocking In method in rock painting, but they are not aware of the name.

In simple terms, "Blocking In" is where the painting begins with colors positioned in flat shapes. When Blocking In is performed, the paints are usually still wet, meaning you should not tamper with it.

This common technique also allows you to alter things to the way you want. You can see the paints and change each color to the one you like with how the shapes are.

When you are satisfied with changing the colors, you need to allow it dry before going over to the subsequent layer.

3. Layering Technique

The layering technique is a continuation of the Blocking In technique. It is done by adding extra colors and more information. In the layering technique, your design is already becoming clearer, and you can see how beautiful it is going to look.

The recommended paint for the layering technique is acrylic because it dries quicker than other oil paints. Meanwhile, if you decide not to do the Blocking In technique, simply recall that you have the option to make your colors have extra depth by painting its layers.

4. Dry Brushing

The dry brush technique represents painting with a brush that is not mixed with water. The brush strokes are rubbed on the rocks, and the outcome is less scratchy.

If you want to change to another color while painting your rock using the dry brush technique, simply rinse the brush and dry off the water from the brush.

The dry brush technique brings measurement and quality to painted rocks.

5. Stippling

This rock painting technique is done by using a flat brush to produce little dots. For instance, you can use a flat brush to make a tree-like dot.

Stippling is majorly used to join colors together and produce a unique design.

6. Wet on Wet

Using the wet on wet rock painting technique makes it simple to mix different paints. It is a very easy technique to use, and beginners can use it without any trouble.

An example of a wet on wet technique is when you want to paint your image's background, but it is still wet. This technique requires you to start painting the foreground first before painting the other sides.

7. Acrylic Pouring Technique

The acrylic pouring technique is considered the most fun method of creating abstract art. There are several different methods to engage in acrylic pouring.

One of the most common techniques of acrylic pouring is referred to as the dirty pour. This technique works when the pour paint colors in layers are placed in a cup and applied on the rocks.

8. Watercolor or Washing Technique

The watercolor or washing technique can be done by dipping acrylic paint into the water to form a translucent look. The produced look or outcome is similar to a watercolor look.

9. Alcohol Inks on Rocks Method

This is another fun way of painting rocks that produces great results. First of all, alcohol inks are everlasting, and they dry faster than you think.

Meanwhile, it is a great way for beginners to start their rock painting career. All you have to do to make this technique successful is to paint your rock with alcohol inks.

10. Splattering or Flicking Technique

The splattering or flicking rock painting technique works by using a flat wet paintbrush to flick or splash paint on your rock's body.

Some people prefer to use their second hand to tap the brush on the rock to have fantastic spray paint on all the rocks.

The flicking rock painting technique is an amazing method of adding more juice or feeling to your color paint.

11. Mandala Dot Art

The Mandala dot art is a difficult geometric circular form produced by lines. It is another technique associated with rock painting, but it requires a tool to work effectively.

People who use the Mandala Dot Art rock painting technique usually use a detail brush or dotting tool to make this technique successful.

12. Detailing

This rock painting technique focuses on details alone. The detailing technique is considered the last step when carrying out the layering procedures.

It also requires you to use a fine detail brush to apply the last touches to your painted rock to make it beautiful and attractive.

13. Ombre Blending Technique

The ombre blending method is a technique to acquire when working with acrylics. However, the process of learning ombre blending might take some time and consistent practice.

This is because it dries quickly, which is worrisome with lighter paint. Meanwhile, if you use thicker paint, it would be much easier because the drying process is not so fast.

For example, painters can lay color and take another one and place it before using the brush. A flat brush is highly recommended for the ombre blending technique.

14. Soft Gradient Look Technique

This method of rock painting uses a latex makeup sponge to form a soft gradient look. To use this technique, you need to apply the paints to the sponge and dip it in a straight line across the place where you want the ombre effect to begin.

Once done, allow it dry for some minutes before adding another coat. Once again, leave it to dry, and from there, you can use a clean sponge for dipping it to the upper area to close other parts of the rock and blend.

Depending on your choice, you can either add extra coats to cover the rock completely or not.

15. Double-Loading for Blending

The last technique on our list of rock painting techniques is the double leading method. It also allows rock painters to make a gradient look on your rock.

The double leading technique works by taking a few double colors, touching them on the brush edges, and spreading them. Go through the same process once again if you want to paint the other part, and your rock will come out with a beautiful blend line.

Chapter 3

Getting Started with Rock Painting

Basic Tools and Supplies Needed

Acrylic Paint

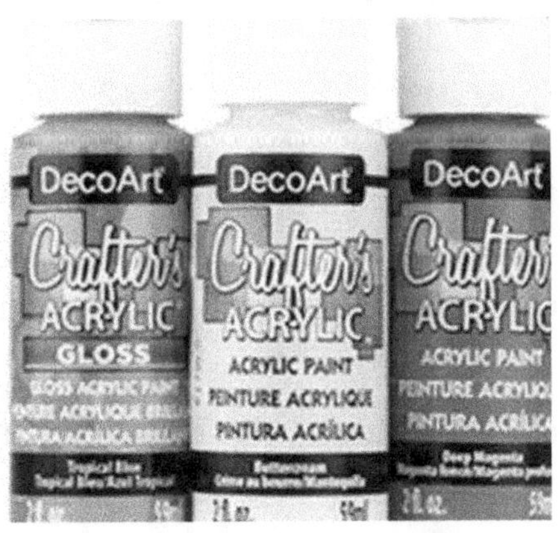

Acrylic paint is a quick-drying paint produced from pigment suspended in acrylic plasticizers, metal soaps, defoamers, silicon oils, and stabilizers.

Acrylic paint will become water-resistant when the liquid content is dried up. The paint is made up of 3 components, namely: Blinder, Vehicle, and Pigment.

Reasons why people love using Acrylic paint

1. While wet, you can clean them using water.

2. Acrylic paints dry very fast. It takes about 12 minutes for thin acrylic paints to dry.

3. They don't have fumes and they have little or no odor.

4. Acrylic paints are not flammable.

5. They can glue to nearly all surfaces

6. They are effective with different painting designs.

Paint Palettes

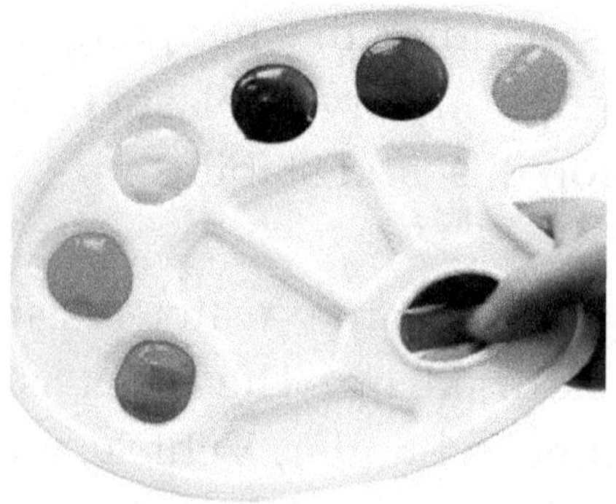

The paint palette is a strong, simple to clean, flat surface where a painter organizes and adds paints. It is an essential tool for painters because it helps to prevent paints from pouring away.

Paint palettes can be made from glass, plastic, wooden palette, and paper.

Plastic paint palette

The plastic paint palette usually includes oils, acrylics, and watercolor. They are designed from thick and high-quality plastics.

Paper palette

Paper palettes are disposable, and they are made from heavy white and smooth paper of different sizes and shapes. It is made to be used only once.

Glass paint palette

This is where it gets tricky with paint palettes. The typical glass paint palette is dangerous, but the safe ones are perfect for acrylics and oils. You can easily mix acrylic paint with the glass type without the fear of having the paint splash on you.

Wooden paint palette

The wooden paint palette is the most popular paint palette used mainly for oils and not acrylics. It is not advisable to be used with acrylics because the wood is rigid, and it will be difficult to erase once it is stained.

Rocks

Rock is a very vital component of rock painting. They come in different sizes and shapes depending on the project you have at hand. Rocks can be found in several areas, including your backyard, beach, and in craft stores.

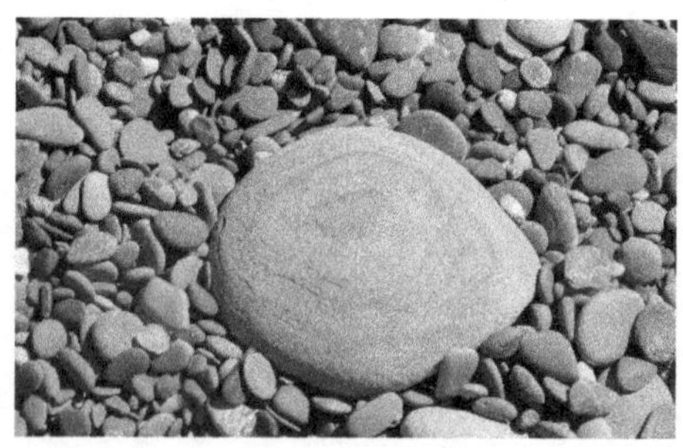

Some rocks are triangle in shape; others can be oval-shaped, flat, smooth, rough, or round. For example, if you want to paint a shark rock, you will need to get a triangular-shaped rock.

Look below to know how to find rocks for your different projects:

1. Your home

Yes. Rocks meant for your rock painting project can be found in your home. If you stay in a rocky area, check your backyard or around your home and locate a suitable rock that will serve your rock painting idea.

2. Art store

If you need a rock for a unique rock painting project and cannot find it within your environment, you can get them from an art store. Several art stores sell rocks for the different rock painting project.

3. Beach

The beach is also another location where you can find a rock for your rock painting project. There are usually tons of rocks on the river banks of beaches. So, if you will be going to the beach, you should take a bag along with you to gather the rocks you need.

Paint Brushes

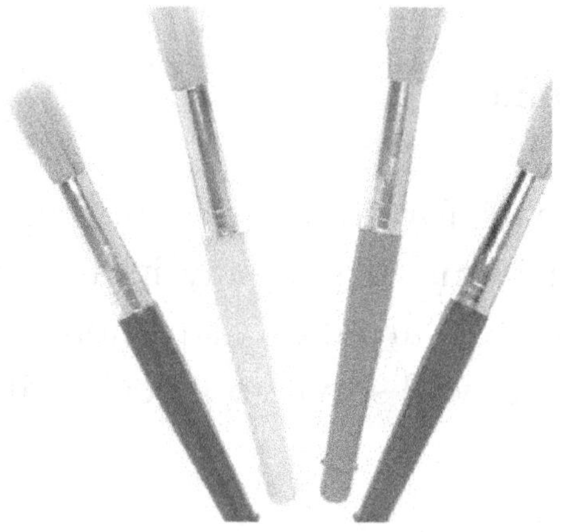

The paintbrush is very efficient in mixing and adding colors. It is also a perfect choice for people looking to use acrylic paints.

Paintbrushes are divided into four different parts, namely:

- **Bristles** – They are also classified as hairs. Bristles are usually synthetic or natural.

- **Crimp** – It is the component of a paintbrush that is glued to its handle.

- **Ferrule** – This is the silver side of the paintbrush that joins with the handle.

- **Handle** – The handle is where you get hold of the paintbrush. They are usually produced from acrylic or wood.

There are up to 8 different paintbrush types majorly used in acrylic painting. The different types of paint brushes are used for one purpose or the other. They include:

- **Pointed round paintbrush**

It is very narrow, and its tip is pointed up. Pointed round paintbrush are often perfect for gentle areas, lines, spotting, retouching, and fine details.

- **Bright paintbrush**

It is a flat paintbrush with curvy edges and small hairs. They are perfect for heavy colors and shortly managed strokes.

- **Round paintbrush**

As the name implies, the round paintbrush is a round brush. The round paintbrush is perfect for many things, including outlining, creating thin lines, sketching, detailed work, and controlled washes.

- **Fan paintbrush**

The fan paintbrush is flat, and its hairs are apart from each other. They are usually used for blending, feathering, and smoothing.

- **Detail round paintbrush**

The detail round paintbrush has a short handle. It also has short hairs, and it is round in shape. The detail round paintbrush also takes more color than you feel, and it is perfect for short strokes and details.

- **Flat paintbrush**

Flat paintbrush has long hairs, and it has a square end shape. It is usually used for washes, impasto, filling wide spaces, and bold strokes. Furthermore, flat paintbrushes can be used for stripes, straight edges, and fine lines.

- **Angular flat paintbrush**

It has flat angled hairs at its edges. It is capable of getting into little areas with tip. What's more, it looks like flat brushes, and it covers many spaces.

- **Filbert paintbrush**

The Filbert paintbrush is oval and flat in shape. It is perfect for sound, rounded ends, and blending.

Markers and Pens

Markers and pens are significant components of rock painting. They are used to draw or design rocks with notes or images. Take a look at the different kinds of markers and pens used in rock painting below.

- **Paint Markers**

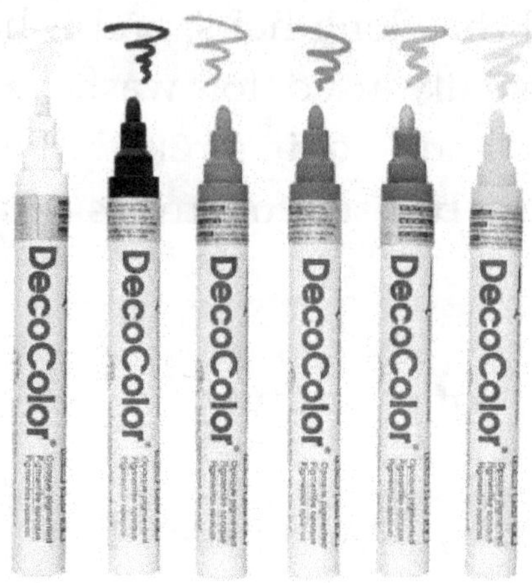

Paint markers are a special type of markers that are usually used to permanently write notes on several surfaces, including rocks, paper, plastic, glass, and rubber.

The inks contained in paint markers are oil-paints that need you to shake their content before painting. The downside to using paint markers is that it contains harmful substances which include toluene and xylene.

Paint markers are not advised to be used in a tight space, with little or no ventilation.

- **Pens for Outlining**

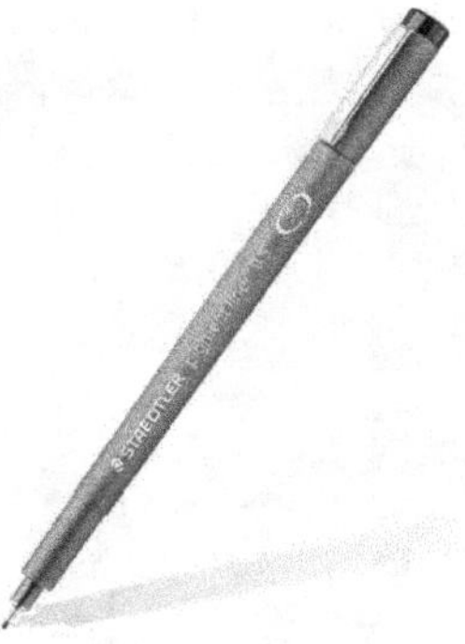

In a rock painting project, you may need to design an image or written words.

What then is recommended for designing or writing notes on rocks? A drawing pen is mostly recommended for writing quotes or sketching an image to be painted.

Different outlining pens in the market vary depending on inks, grips, and tips. The numerous outlining pens also offer different advantages and disadvantages. For instance, one good advantage of using outlining pens is that they dry quickly.

- **Chalk Markers**

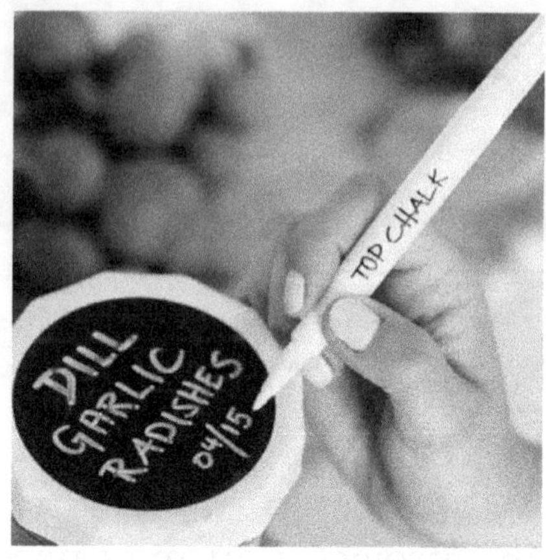

Chalk markers can be used to replace paint pens. They contain liquid ink that creates a chalk-like form when dried.

In comparison with the typical chalk, the chalk markers do not stain. You can use chalk markers to paint layers of colors over the top of another layer.

Chalk markers are mostly used on rocks, glass, chalkboards, plastic, whiteboards, and mirrors. Its ink can be cleaned using water.

- **Chalk Crayons**

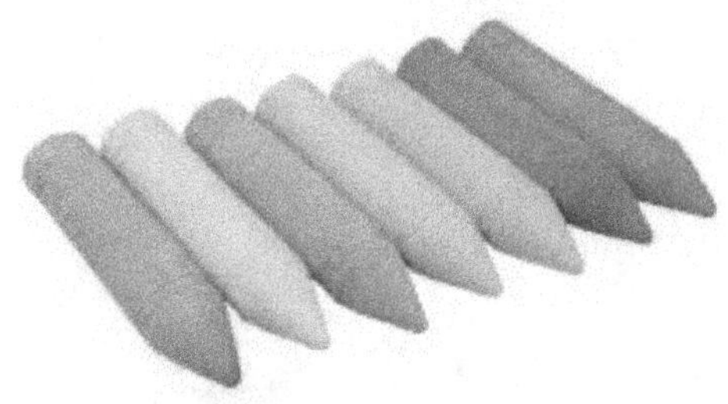

Chalk crayons are suitable for several surfaces like rocks, whiteboards, wood, and glass. They are not like the regular chalks that easily drop their contents.

They are also perfect for children who are looking to paint rocks. Instead of giving your kids the typical acrylic paint, you can give them chalk crayons, especially if you won't be around painting rocks with them.

Chalk crayons do not create a messy surface when used, and it can be easily wiped off with a wet cloth.

Dotting Tools

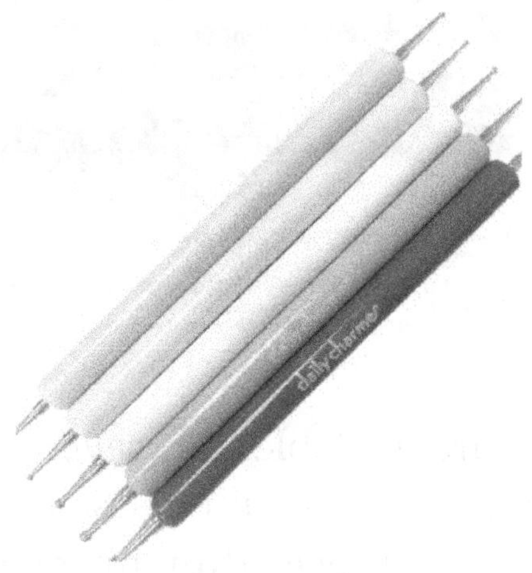

Dotting tools are unique tools that are used for painting various dot mandala sizes on different surfaces.

How can I use dotting tools to paint dot mandala surfaces?

1. Put the tip of the dotting tool into any of your chosen paint. You don't need to dip the entire dotting tool because you only need a little amount of paint.

2. With your hands, position the dotting tool vertically to the rock surface.

3. Lastly, press the dotting tool on the rock surface. Don't hold the dotting tool on your rock surface for too long so as not to spill too much paint on the rock.

Once done using the dotting tool, you will have to clean them. You can do so through the following ways:

1. Use a paper napkin to clean the dotting tool because you will most likely find a stain on the edge of the tool.

2. For hard removal of paint, you should dip the paper napkin into hot water for 16 seconds before wiping the hardened paint.

3. Do not make the mistake of using baby wipes, alcohol-based paints, and rubbing alcohol to clean your stained dotting tool unless advised.

Rock Sealers

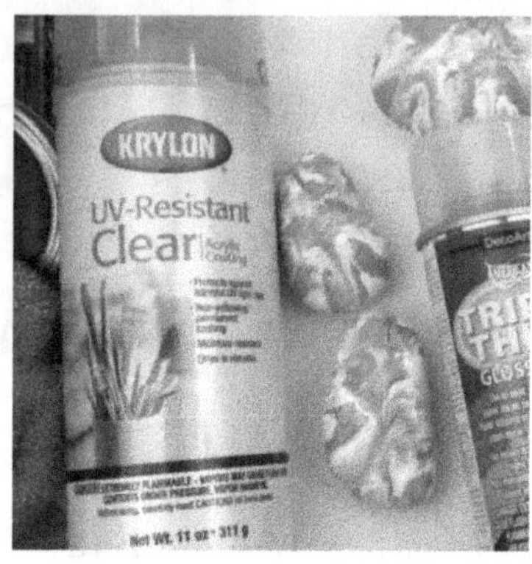

Rock sealers are recommended solutions that help you preserve your rock against moisture or any outdoor toxic substance that can damage your painted rock. Rock sealers are often used whenever the rock is placed outside the home.

Sealers also help prevent your painted rocks from storms, dust, rain, and other harsh elements. So, how do we seal a painted rock? The steps include:

1. **Leaving your painted rock to dry**

After you have completed painting your rock, you should leave it to dry before the sealing process begins.

Under normal circumstances, your painted rock should dry at the end of 24 hours.

Sealing your rock while it is still wet can damage your rock paint, and you wouldn't want that to happen because it will render all your earlier efforts useless.

2. Select a good sealer

The next step is for you to select a good sealer. You can choose to use a brush on sealer or spray sealer.

If you want to keep your painted rock indoors, then a brush on sealer is recommended. However, if your painted rock is meant for outdoor decoration, you should use a spray sealer.

Selecting a good sealer is also dependent on the type of paint you used in decorating your rock. But this shouldn't worry you because different paints usually have their sealers.

3. Position the spray sealer

Since we will be focusing on outdoor sealing, you will need to get a spray sealer and not a brush-on sealer.

Now, you have to position the spray sealer the right way before you begin spraying your painted rock. Most people usually make the mistake of holding the spray sealer very close to the painted rock.

The right way to position the spray sealer is within 9 – 12 inches away from the rock. This will produce a very smooth and clear surface rather than a rough surface.

4. Spray, Spray, Spray

Begin spraying your painted rock gently to produce a light coat. At the initial stage, don't try to make a thick coat.

You can get a thin coat by spraying 3 times after the first 2 coats have dried. While spraying your rock, ensure you spray the rear side, the front side, and every side you see.

5. Seal the rocks

Once done creating a thin and thick coat on your rock, you need to keep them away from the sun until it is no longer wet.

The best way to be sure that your sprayed rock is dried is that it won't smell any longer.

Once dried, you can take your painted and sealed rock outside and show it to the world.

Choosing and Preparing the Rocks

Before you start painting rocks, you have to choose and prepare the rocks you will use. Once you have your rock ready, the painting exercise is only but some minutes away from completion.

How do you choose and prepare rocks?

The steps below show the various ways you can choose and prepare rocks for your rock painting exercise:

1. **Find the right rock**

You need to find the right rock that will fit perfectly with your rock painting project. There are tons of rocks to choose from; however, you need to make sure you select the right one.

Rocks come in different sizes and shapes, and you can choose them depending on the design you plan to create. For example, an oval-shaped rock is used to paint an Easter egg rock.

Different rocks can be selected from the riverside, your backyard, or a craft store.

2. Wash your rock

Rocks picked up from your backyard, and the riverside is always filled with dirt. So, what do you need to do to make them clean? You have to wash the dirty rocks with soap and water before leaving them to dry.

Simply place your rock under running water, rub some soap and use your fingers to wash away the dirt you find on it.

Meanwhile, if you bought a rock from the craft store and are waxy, you need to boil the rocks or use a nail polish remover to clean them for use.

3. Smoothen them if needed

Perhaps you purchased or collected a rough rock, but you need a smooth one for your rock painting project. Well, not to worry because there are tools you can use to make your rock smooth.

If you are unsure of what to use to make your rock smooth, you can contact your local craft store to give you the tool that smoothens rocks.

4. Paint

Once you have completed the entire process above, your rock is then ready to get painted. Before you forget, ensure you allow the paint to dry before moving to the next steps. This will prevent you from ruining your rock.

Painting Basics and Tips

Paints are needed to decorate rocks, so you must be careful while using the right paint. The most recommended paint for your rock painting project is acrylic paint because they are always proven to dry very fast.

In fact, acrylic paints are also recommended for beginners. There are some basic rules of thumb you need to know before using paints on your rocks. These principles include:

1. Choose your paint color quickly

Most paint colors like acrylic often dry quickly, so you need to decide on the color you are using very fast before they dry.

If you are fast with your decision, you can easily erase a paint mistake you make on your rock. There isn't much time to debate with acrylic paint, unlike when you are using oil paints.

2. Mix colors the right way

You should be able to mix colors well if there is any need for it. Mixing colors are usually done on palettes. It is often advised that you experiment with mixing colors before you take it to your main rock painting project.

You can check the step by step method of mixing custom colors after the next sub-heading.

3. Choose a color you are OK with

Do not always follow the crowd and use the color they are using. If many people are using a particular color, it does not mean it will go down well with your rock painting design.

If a paint color dries too fast, you may just want to switch to another that takes more time to dry. Although it may take extra time, it is still a good way to avoid mistakes and regret.

4. Use quality paints

Less quality paints can ruin your rock and your rock painting design. Even though you may be within a budget, if you choose to spend more money on quality paints, you won't have to spend money later.

Quality paints will bring out the bright color of your rock design, and it will give you every reason to smile.

5. Don't use paints that will stain your brush permanently

It is essential not to use paints that will be difficult to wash away even after many attempts. If you want to buy paint, ensure you ask the seller what paint type it is and how long it takes before it can be erased from a paintbrush.

Choosing Colors to Use

One of the important ways to have a beautiful painted rock is choosing the right colors. Color paints for your rocks can come in red, green, yellow, pink, blue, and other colors.

While choosing the right color can make your rock beautiful, selecting the wrong ones can make your rocks less attractive. But how do we choose the colors to use?

1. Select colors that match your rock painting project

You wouldn't want to choose a color that does not match your rock painting project because it won't come out well. For example, if you want to design a beautiful flower rock, you are not expected to choose colors such as black because it would ruin your flower rock.

Instead, use colors such as yellow and pink because they will make your flowers very attractive.

2. **Use bright and dark colors depending on the rock painting project**

Some rock painting project requires you to use bright colors, while others may need you to use dark colors. So, depending on the rock painting project at hand, you can choose to use any color options.

3. **Don't settle for less**

If the craft store doesn't have the color that will make your rock painting project beautiful, don't buy the ones available.

It is better to suspend your rock painting exercise than be desperate and end up using colors that will ruin your rock painting project.

Mixing Custom Colors

Have you ever bought the wrong color shade and the store didn't accept it back? Or, have you bought paint, and the color is not what you thought it was? Well, don't be scared.

As a painter or non-painter, you can easily mix the custom colors with a few other ingredients to create the color you intended to have. While mixing the custom colors, ensure you do not discard the wrong colors you bought because it can still be used to mix custom paints. Therefore, it will further save you the stress of having to pay for new paint.

If you are still looking for the right ways to mix custom paint colors, you should know the materials and tools needed to make the process smooth.

Tools and Materials needed for mixing custom colors

Before you mix custom colors, you need to know the colors and materials needed to make the process successful. Below are some materials you need to mix custom colors:

- White paint

- Craft colorants

- Color wheel

NOTE – The outcome of the custom color mixing is dependent on the first colors you purchased. It will also be dependent on your experience level in mixing colors and the colorants available to be used.

You also need to get an excellent paint base because it will make the mixed color either dark or bright.

How to mix custom colors

Rough or proper custom color mixing will have the final say on how it will look. For that reason, you need to be aware of the methods to create the unique colors you want. Look below for the right ways on how to mix custom colors:

1. **Lighten Up the Color**

The is the first step and most crucial technique needed to mix custom colors properly. It would be best if you had white paint to make the paint color lighter. Without white paint, you won't be able to achieve a lighter paint color.

The amount of white paint you need is dependent on how pale you want it to look and how dark the paint color is. However, it will take a reasonably large quantity of white paint for you to notice the brightness in the paint color.

In some instances, you may only need to add a little amount of the paint color to the white paint, and not vice-versa. Making a color light up is an inexpensive way to "stretch" paint. This is mostly because white paint is not costly to purchase.

Lightening up your color paint shouldn't be a tedious task because it can be performed in some minutes if you have all the materials needed.

2. Darken the Color

The subsequent step to mix custom colors successfully is to darken the paint color. Adding some gray or black craft colorant will darken a color.

You need to use a black craft colorant if you want to darken a color that is already deep. On the other hand, use a gray craft colorant if you are darkening lighter colors.

You require a little amount of black colorant to darken a pastel noticeably. However, if you need a unique type of change, use a sufficient amount of colorant.

While darkening a color, it is advisable to stay within two shades of the initial color. You will also get frustrated when you try to change a pale sky blue color into a dark navy blue color.

3. Strengthen the Color

For your custom paint color to be bright, you have to include an extra-base color. For instance, if you want to brighten up a tan color, you need to add a few orange or yellow colors. Also, to lighten up a sage green color added, green color is needed.

4. Tone Down the Color

Adding 2 colors lying openly across each other on the paint color will reduce the color's high nature.

For example, violent colors will nullify and counteract a bright yellow color. Thereby, making the lightened yellow color to look more refined and smoother.

5. Alter the Hue

You also have the option to change color undertones, hues, and temperatures. For instance, a green color's intensity can increase when you add yellow color to it.

On the other hand, the same green color's intensity can be reduced by adding blue color. Red colors can change into violet, even without adding a blue color.

Do not forget that difficult custom paint colors such as beiges, greys, and browns are more challenging to modify because they have too many hues.

Meanwhile, more comfortable colors such as yellow, blue, green, and others are not difficult to change. Also, ensure you practice or rehearse in a little container to know the color mixture's outcome before you take it into a large container.

This will save you a lot of things, including color wastage and money.

NOTE – While mixing custom colors, make sure it is stirred well for the desired effect to come out. Moreover, ensure you mix sufficient color paint and purchase a large quantity of paint prior to the exercise, so you don't need to suspend the process to buy paint.

Most importantly, you cannot re-create custom paint colors after its mixture. Finally, your mixed custom color deserves a beautiful name, so give it one.

Transferring Designs onto Rocks

Do you have a shape or image design you want to paint on the rock, but you cannot use freehand drawing? Well, there are different steps you can take to transfer designs onto rocks.

Transferring designs onto rocks is one way to beautify painted rocks and make them look beautiful.

For this first step, we would be using the following materials and tools:

- Carbon paper

- Glue

- Pen

- Cutting machine / Scissors

- Wet brush

- Tape

- Rock

- Black acrylic paint

Create a Stencil

A stencil is not the most likely solution to transferring designs onto rocks, but it might just work. The downsides to using a stencil are that the paint would stain when the stencil is raised, or the pen would slip.

Overall, when using a stencil, always have patience unless you want to spoil all the designs you hope to get. For others, they usually use a sketch.

Cut and Glue

After sketching or creating a stencil, the next step is to cut off the designs. Now, if you have a cutting machine, the process would be made much easier. Otherwise, you can use scissors to cut the sketch or stencil.

Meanwhile, while cutting with scissors, ensure you are careful enough to cut what is needed to be transferred to the rock. Once you have cut out the designs successfully, you will need to glue them onto the rock.

Decoupage glue is a good example of glue you can use to fix your designs onto your rock. When you glue the design onto your rock, you can either choose to leave it outside to dry or cover it with some varnish layers.

Use Carbon Paper

This is one of the best ways of transferring designs onto rocks. For example, you can sketch a design on paper and easily transfer it onto your rock. To get the best outcome out of this technique, you should use it with a flatter rock.

First of all, paint the body of the rock and leave it to dry. It is usually best to leave the rock to dry all through the night. Meanwhile, if the paint is yet to dry, you may get small black carbon speckles on the paint.

For Acrylics paint, it creates a glossy hard surface when it has dried. When this happens, simply erase the black speckles off using a wet brush.

The carbon paper technique works when you cut out the design and tape of the carbon paper. Ensure the carbon paper is joined with its carbon side down. Many people make mistakes at this point, but it is essential to be careful by cutting out the design and taping the carbon paper.

Proceed to tape the two designs onto the rock and move on to the top of the design lines using a pen. Paint artists can use an easy ball-point pen for this process. However, you are not restricted to only using a ball-point pen, as you can try out other options.

Once the above process is done, simply remove the design and you would have transferred your design onto the rock successfully.

Another method of transferring design images onto rocks can be done using nail polish and white or black laser print-outs.

Materials needed to transfer design images onto rocks:

1. Nail polish

2. PC with any photo editor

3. Laser printer

4. Acrylic varnish

5. Alcohol-containing liquid (E.g., it could be rubbing alcohol, vodka, or cologne).

The steps include the following:

1. Locate a nice design image, flip it horizontally using any photo editor and reduce its size to fit on your rock

Most photo editors usually use Gimp to flip images. Once you are done flipping your preferred image in Gimp, proceed to copy it to the Word document program and reduce its size to fit on your rock *(NB: Most people use their natural eye to reduce the size of the image on Word).*

But if your preferred image does not have words in it, then there is no need to flip it horizontally. The design will simply look on the revered side after you have transferred onto your rock with words in it.

2. **Print out the image on a white and black laser printer**

The subsequent step to follow is to print out the image on a white and black laser printer. Then cut out only the printed words or design you need from the paper.

All other parts of the paper should be kept aside once you have successfully cut out the part you need.

3. **Put nail polish on the rock**

Using clear nail polish, apply it directly to your rock's body. When done, please leave it to dry completely before moving to the next step.

You can dry it overnight or place it outdoors to dry in a short period under the hot sun.

4. **Use any alcohol comprising liquid and place an image in it for 3 or 5 seconds**

You can purchase cheap alcohol from your local drug store to use for this process. As long as the alcohol has liquid inside, you can easily use it.

Examples of common liquid alcohol used for this process include cologne or vodka. Pour a little amount of the alcohol into a bowl. Then take up your image and dip it in the alcohol for about 3 or 5 seconds long.

Do not exceed 5 seconds, or you will be making a big mistake.

5. Ensure the image is facing down on your rock

After dipping the image inside the alcohol for not more than 5 seconds, make sure the image is facing down on your rock.

Leave it that way for 20 or 30 seconds before peeling the image off the rock. This will lead to the word or the design sticking to your rock.

6. Put a coat of acrylic varnish so that the design will not erase

Usually, the design after peeling off the rock's image will last for a long without using an acrylic varnish. However, if you want the design on your rock to last for several years to come, then a coat of acrylic varnish is needed.

After applying a coat of acrylic varnish to your rock, you should leave it to dry so that the design can be fixed on your rock permanently.

7. Finished process

At this point, you have concluded the process of transferring designs onto your rock successfully. The most challenging aspect of transferring designs onto rocks is choosing the right design or image, as the other process takes nothing more than 12 minutes to complete.

A Short message from the Author:

Hey, I hope you are enjoying the book? I would love to hear your thoughts!

Many readers do not know how hard reviews are to come by and how much they help an author.

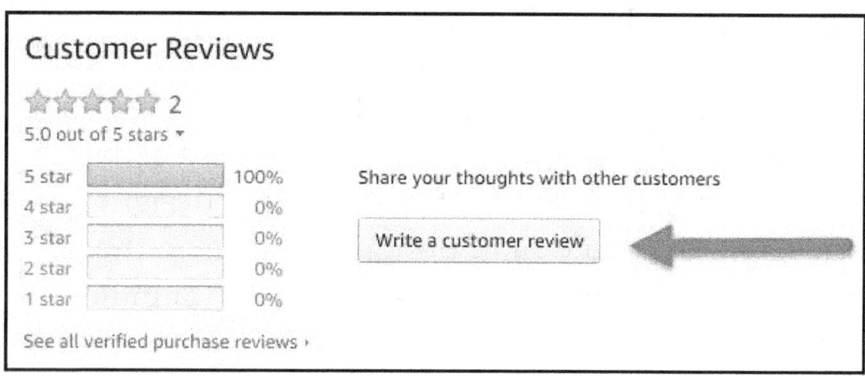

I would be incredibly grateful if you could take just 60 seconds to write a short review on Amazon, even if it is a few sentences!

\>> Click here to leave a quick review

Thanks for the time taken to share your thoughts!

Chapter 4

Fixing Rock Painting Mistakes

During your rock painting journey, there is every chance you might make mistakes that can ruin your painted rock. However, we will be discussing how to fix the common rock painting mistakes that actually make your work look poor.

Rock painting mistakes do not only apply when painting rocks. Other sections that record mistakes when rock painting is ongoing are when drawing or sealing aspects.

Even as an experienced rock painter, there must have been a time you made a mistake. It is inevitable, especially when you are just starting your rock painting career.

We have compiled several ways to fix rock painting mistakes on drawing, painting, and sealing, respectively.

How to fix drawing mistakes on painted rocks

Drawing on painted rocks is usually done using paint pens. However, if you made a grave or little mistake, you can do the following to correct them:

1. Go ahead and paint the inner part of the outline. Increase its size to close the outline. After that, sketch the edge of the painted areas where you made a mistake.

Meanwhile, if you want to remove the paint pens mistake on your rock, you should look out for some necessary tips below:

-   Endeavor to paint the base layer once more. But if you did not notice any positive change even after painting the base layer two times, you will have to paint the rock with the sketch's color. This process can be done on other projects as well.

    It is important to always use smooth rocks while painting rocks. However, if you are using a rough rock to paint, you might not use paint pens to draw on it because of the rough layers or the lumps. In the meantime, here are some solutions you can consider when painting on rough rocks:

a. Sand the rock.

b. Paint the lower part of the rock with a thick gesso paint primer.

c. Get wood filler.

Tips for preventing rock painting mistakes when using painting pens

Here are some tips to follow when you want to use painting pens on rocks:

1. Endeavor to sketch a complex design using a pencil

Alternatively, you can also use graphite paper to place all your designs. This is a crucial tip because it allows you to have a picture of the design you want to create.

Instead of using a pen for this process, use a pencil to draw the design because it can quickly be cleared and re-drawn.

When you have gotten the full sketch or outline of the design you want to create on your rock, it would be tough to make a costly mistake.

2. Select rocks that will fit the design task

Why trouble or disturb yourself with a rough rock when you can get a smooth rock? Although smooth rocks might cost you some penny, it is still better than getting a rough rock that will cause you problems.

It is challenging to use paint pens on rough rocks because you won't paint on all its sides.

However, with a smooth rock, all these problems, including paint pens issues, will not come up. But if it's a rough rock you need to complete your project, then go for it.

3. Wipe away the sketch or outline to some extent to totally cover it

Not minding the paint color, you need to slightly erase the sketch or outline you have created for your rock painting exercise. This will help you to be able to cover your work.

4. Do not make attempts to hand letter rocks

5. Don't try to be perfect; simply make progress

Instead of trying to be perfect when using paint pens on your rock, keep trying your best. There is nothing wrong with making mistakes at the initial stage. Meanwhile, as you progress and gain experience, your mistake level will significantly drop, leading you to become an expert or a professional.

How to fix the main rock painting mistakes

If you make a mistake while painting rocks, here are some solutions you can follow to fix them:

1. Wash away the paint immediately with a slightly dipped cloth using water.

Luckily, suppose you wanted to paint in one area of your rock and ended up painting in another area entirely; in that case, you can easily fix the issue by washing away the paint immediately.

Make sure you dip a cloth into the water a bit before using it to clean the paint on your rock.

2. Allow it dry before scrapping its body

Another method of fixing rock painting mistakes is to leave the painted rock to dry entirely before scrapping the paint away from the rock.

Alongside the first, this technique is also widely used because it has been proven to work effectively.

However, there is still a downside to scraping off paint from a rock.

The major challenge you may experience is that you might end up spoiling the rock, meaning you won't be able to use the rock anymore. By scraping off the paint from the rock, you may render the rock rough and damage its smooth texture.

3. Use dawn dish soap on dried painted rock

If you allow the paint to dry on the rock, you can still remove it without scrapping its body. Another method of removing dried painted rock is to use dawn dish soap on a slightly dipped paper towel to rub on the rock.

This method is not common, but rock paintings experts have confirmed that it works just fine, hence, the suggestion.

4. Nail polish remover

A nail polish remover can also work to remove rock painting mistakes. Look below to see how nail polish remover can work to erase rock painting mistakes:

- Get a cotton swab.

- Pour a little amount of nail polish remover on the cotton swab.
- Slowly but effectively remove the paint mistakes.
- Once done, the painted rock will be free from its created mistakes, and you can use the rock to paint once more.

5. Use Goof Off

Although its content smell very bad, Goof Off is still an effective rock paint removal option you can try out.

Follow the steps below to use Goof Off to remove rock painting mistakes:

- Leave your painted rock to dry off.
- Apply the Goof Off product directly on your dried painted rock.
- Use a slightly wet cloth to wipe away the dried paint from the rock.
- Wait for some time, and you will see the impressive changes made to your painted rock.

6. Repaint the lower part of the rock to a color that you can't remove

Assuming you make a mistake when painting your rock, simply repaint your rock's base part to the color you are sure will not remove.

This technique works just fine, but it should only be done when the mistake happens at an early stage.

7. Sand it off

If you have a bare rock and you ended up making a mistake while painting, you can easily sand it off. However, this technique does not work all the time. It will work well in some cases, and the mistake cleared from your rock, while in other cases, the rock will become worse.

Generally, sand off method or paint removal works best on light-colored and smooth rocks.

8. Use a paint eraser

The final technique you can use to remove rock painting mistakes is a paint eraser. Paint erasers can be bought in different craft stores or on Amazon.

As a matter of fact, paint erasers work when the paint is still wet. So, when you make a mistake while painting, immediately use the paint eraser and remove the paint mistake while still wet.

If you try to use the paint eraser on dried rock paint, you will only damage the rock.

How to prevent rock painting mistakes

It is not all about fixing rock painting mistakes; you should also know how to prevent the mistakes so that you won't be spending money or time looking for solutions.

Follow the detailed list below to know how to stop rock painting mistakes from happening:

1. Try using other items like toothpicks or even your finger rather than markers, brushes, or pens.
2. Endeavor to attempt using several pens, markers, and paints. Don't always use a particular paint type. Although they will not react the same way to your rocks, it is proper to know which one works best for you. It will also help you make

little or no mistakes when you finally decide to paint rocks.

3. Research and test out new things before heading for your rock painting project. Therefore, if you must make a mistake, do it at the testing stage before hitting the major rock painting project.

How to fix sealant mistakes

The last rock painting mistake you can make while the painting process is ongoing is with the seal. However, we have compiled some solutions you can try out to fix sealant mistakes. See below:

1. Scrape it off

In some cases, you will see that a sealant has cracked; what then do you do? Fortunately, a cracked sealant can easily be removed by using a small metal spatula or sharp equipment.

While it may take some time to scrape the sealant off the rock's body, it will certainly work. This technique for fixing sealant mistakes is not a fast one, and only an enduring and committed individual can do it.

2. Use your fingers

Yes. Fingers can also help in fixing sealant mistakes. While there may be doubters, it will surprise you to see how fingers work exceptionally well to remove sealant mistakes.

Meanwhile, if you choose to use your fingers to remove your rock sealant mistakes, ensure you do it while the sealer on your rock is still wet. A dried sealant will be almost impossible to be removed with fingers.

If the sealant is dried, opt instead to use a small metal sharp tool.

3. Use cotton swab

When sealing your rock and you notice a mistake after the sealant has dried, you can use a cotton swab to remove it.

The cotton swab should be used with a little amount of nail polish remover. So, apply a little amount of nail polish remover on the cotton swab and begin to remove the dried sealant on your rock.

However, it is important to note that while undergoing this process of sealant removal, your rock's base layer and paint will also be removed. This means you have to do this process lightly, else you would not like the outcome.

    4. Use a brush and water

Brush and water also work very well in removing sealant mistakes on a rock. But, it is only efficient when the sealant is still wet.

Now, if you are applying the sealant on a rock when the paint is yet to dry, simply dip a paper towel into water and cover it around a brush. This is where the work begins. You should clean the sealant on the painted rock with a wet paper towel.

Just watch to see how the sealant will be removed from the affected rock area. Once removed, you can also take the step to reseal it once more.

However, note that this solution doesn't work all the time. Sadly, your rock paint may also get removed alongside the sealer when using this process. But in most cases, expect a positive outcome.

How to prevent seal painting mistakes

Instead of making sealing mistakes, why not be aware of the steps to take to prevent sealing mistakes on your rock? Here they are:

1. Leave the seal to dry

One of the steps to take to prevent sealing mistakes is to leave the seal to dry off. In some instances, the sealed paint should be left to dry for 1 day. Other times, you can leave it to dry for 3 days.

The time difference that allows you to leave the seal to dry completely depends on the seal you used and the rock.

2. Cover paint, markers, and water-based pens with a water sealant

Covering your markers, water-based pens, and paints with a water sealant help prevent seal painting mistakes.

ModPodge is a perfect example of a water-friendly sealant covering markers, water-based pens, and paints on rocks. A water-sealant is more like a small layer, and with one swipe, leave it to dry.

3. Use multiple sealant types

You can use many sealant types for your rock to find out which one works best for you. For example, you can use spray sealants or polyurethane to know which one of the two will work for your rock with little or no mistake.

Every rock has its required sealant that will probably not have any fault. If you are confused, you can ask the craft store owner or an experienced rock painter.

4. Read the sealant instruction

After purchasing a water-based sealant from the craft store or any other art store, it is important to always read its instruction before using it on your rock.

If the sealant's instruction does not indicate you add a heavy coat, do not add it unless you want to make a mistake. On the other hand, if the sealant instruction requires you to do one thing or the other while sealing your rock, endeavor to do it without hesitation.

5. Learn from your mistake

Usually, mistakes are bound to happen, so don't always feel bad when you make a sealant mistake at the beginning of your rock painting career.

Instead, learn from your sealant mistake so that you won't make the same mistake again when you decide to seal your rock later.

Chapter 5

Rock Painting Design Ideas

Have you ever thought of how amazing it will look to create beautiful rock painting designs? Anyone can create rock painting designs. The idea is an essential thing that is needed to create an attractive rock painting design.

Meanwhile, as fun as it is, creating a rock painting design can be challenging, especially for beginners. You need to have some level of creativity to create a rock painting design that serves different purposes.

If you find it difficult to create several rock painting designs, do not worry because we have compiled 20 different rock painting design ideas suitable for both kids and adults.

Additionally, the 20 rock painting design ideas listed in this chapter are suitable for beginners. Check them out below:

Flower

Flowers are used to portray beauty, and colorful flowers can undoubtedly attract the attention of both kids and adults alike.

In fact, painted rock flowers can be used to decorate gardens, homes, and even schools. Why not get into the excitement of painting rocks with flowers to beautify your household?

Supplies

- Rocks
- Little acrylic paint brushes
- Decoart Americana Acrylics in Lamp, Lilac Meadow, Magenta, and Summer Squash

How to paint flower rocks

Before commencing the process of painting your flower rocks, ensure you thoroughly wash your rocks and leave them to dry.

You won't be able to paint your flower rocks effectively if your rocks are wet. Therefore, you need to allow it dry (possibly overnight or under the sun) before you start painting.

Another point to note is that while painting, always leave your paint to fully dry before entering the next step or changing to a whole different color.

How to paint a pink zinnia flower rock

1. Mix a little amount of black color and orchid color in a bowl.
2. Draw or paint a small dot in the middle of the rock.
3. Proceed to paint 4 long petals in the orchid color
4. Paint 4 long petals in orchid color for the second time.
5. For the third time, paint 4 petals in orchid color (This will produce 12 petals for every flower).

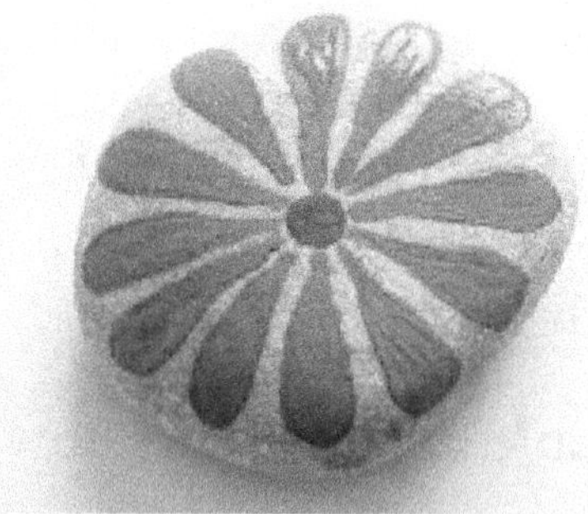

6. Put the paint brush's tip into summer squash and draw small dots in the middle dot.

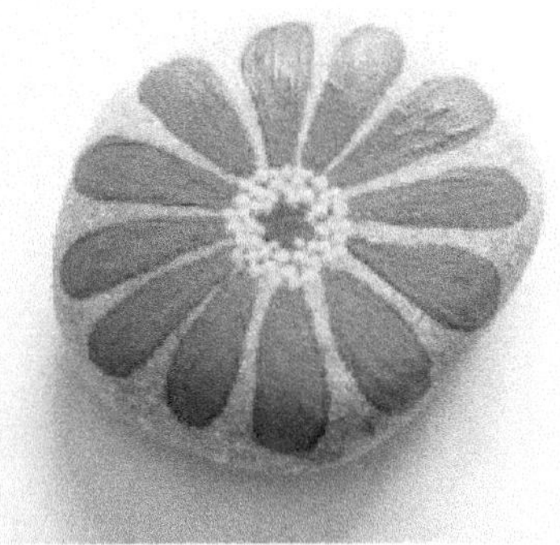

7. Keep on drawing in the sphere until you like the looks of the pink zinnia flower rock.

How to paint a yellow zinnia flower rock

1. Mix a small amount of black and summer squash color.
2. Then paint a little dot in the middle of the rock.
3. Proceed to paint 4 long petals in summer squash.
4. In the same vein, also paint 4 long petals in summer squash.
5. Paint the same thing once again until you get 12 petals for every flower.

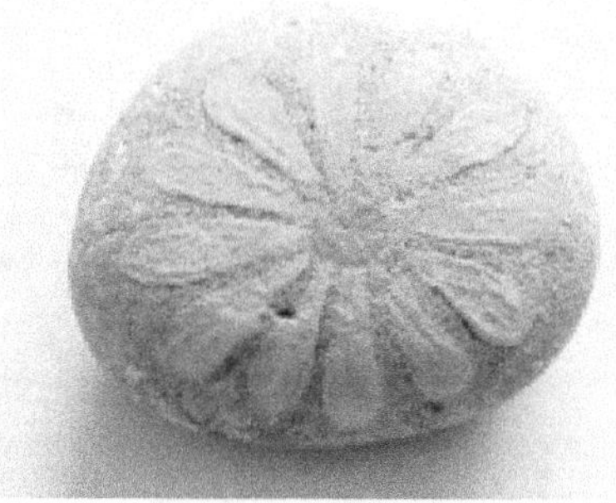

6. Subsequently, using magenta color, paint the bottom part of every petal.
7. With your paintbrush, put the tip into your summer squash and draw small dots in the center dot.
8. Keep the process ongoing until you have gotten what you like.

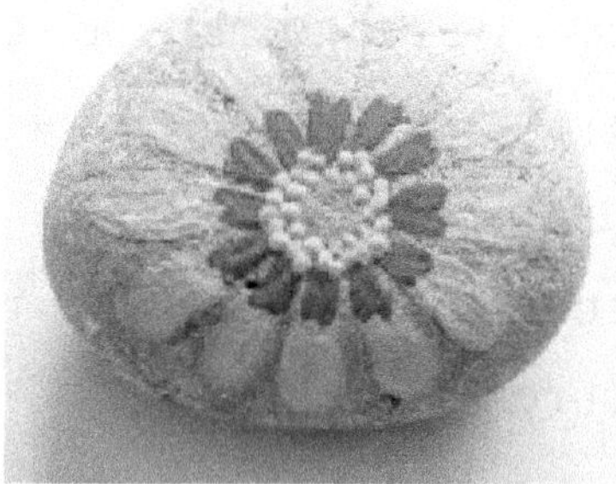

How to paint a purple zinnia flower rock

1. Mix a little amount of black and magenta color.

2. Then paint a minor dot in the middle of the rock.

3. As you have with other zinnia flower rock process, also paint 4 long petals in magenta on 3 occasions until you achieve 12 petals for every flower.

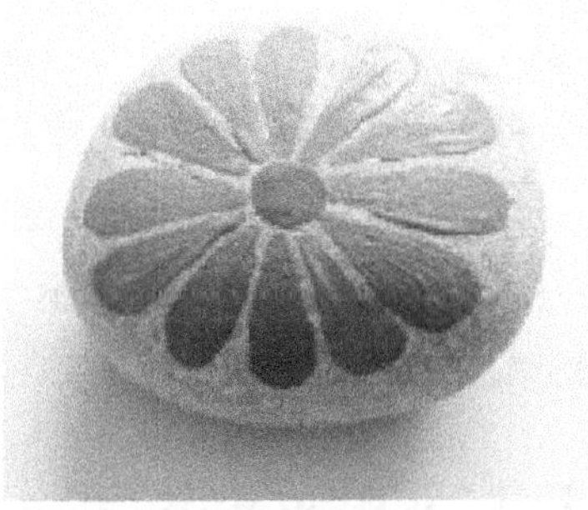

4. Put the edge of your paintbrush into a summer squash color.

5. Draw or paint small dots in the center dot.

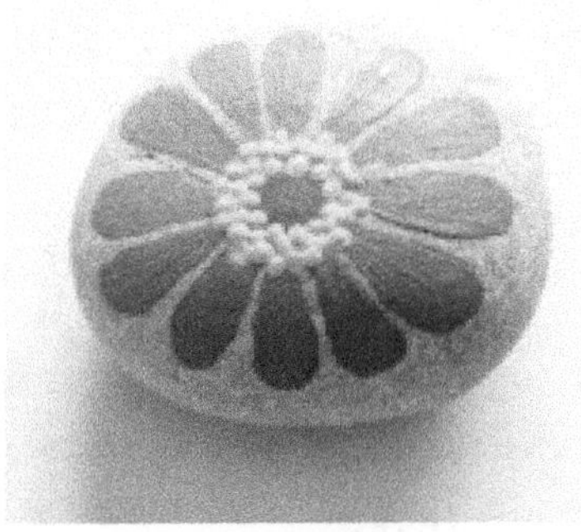

6. Carry on the process until you are satisfied with the rock's looks.

Viola, you have painted your flower rock successfully. You can now take your painted flower rock and position it in your home, garden, or art school.

Bee

The second rock painting design idea ideal for beginners are bee painted rocks. One exciting aspect of this rock painting idea is that it is easy to do, and not too many materials are needed.

It is also ideal for both adults and kids. Once painted, it can be used to decorate your household. Bee rocks are painted to celebrate world bee day, which is usually celebrated on May 20th every year.

As we all know, bees are essential in our existence as human beings and also help in agricultural yield. They produce honey, which humans consume worldwide.

Supplies

- Rock
- Black and yellow aristo markers
- White acrylic paint

How to paint bee rock

Suppose you want to celebrate world bee day or make your kids and others around you happy, you can decide to paint bee rocks. Follow the steps below to make this possible:

1. Wash your rock with little soap and allow the rock to dry.
2. Next, use your white acrylic paint to paint your rock. Once done, also leave the white acrylic paint to dry on the rock.

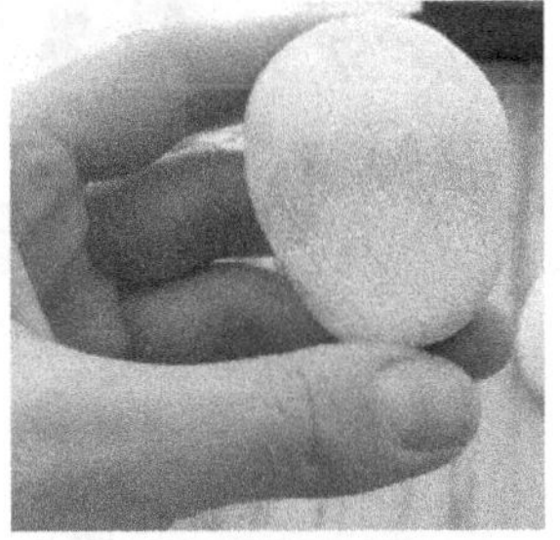

3. Take up your yellow aristo marker and draw some horizontal lines across your rock's body.
4. Do a similar thing using your black, yellow aristo marker as well.

5. You can include a few attractive and delightful personalities to the bee rock by drawing wings, smiles, or eyes using a white marker.

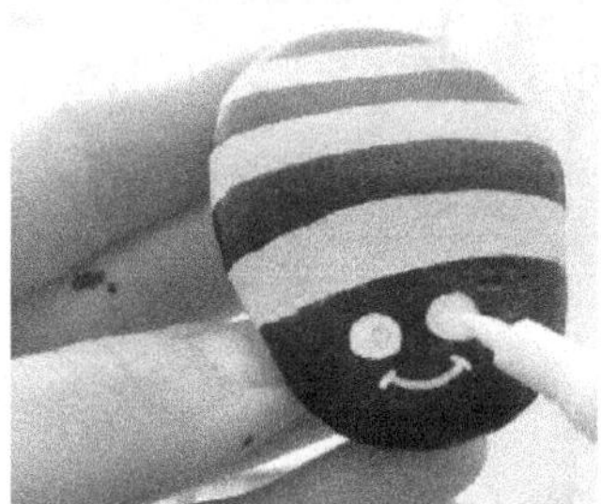

6. Conclude the bee rock painting design by placing attractive flowers on the paper.

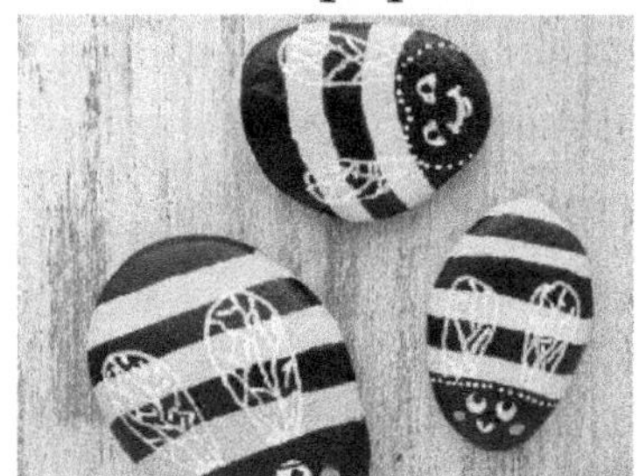

Fish

The fish painted rock project is a fun way to begin your rock painting career. It is perfect for beginners because it joins simple painting skills with the simplicity of drawing while using a pen.

A fish painted rock can be used to display the art of animals. It can also serve other functions that are significant to our existence as humans.

Supplies

- A smooth rock (The rock must be smooth and not rough, or else you won't get the best fish rock design)
- White posca pen
- Clear spray sealer
- Paintbrushes
- Purple shade or Glitterific paint
- Black and additional fine tip posca paint pen
- Color shift blue-violet flash paint
- Color shift aqua flash paint

Follow the steps below to learn how to do the fish paint rock successfully:

1. Wash your clean and smooth rock and allow it to dry completely.
2. Squash a little amount of the color shift aqua flash paint on your rock.

3. With your black posca pen, draw the type of fish you want on your rock's surface.

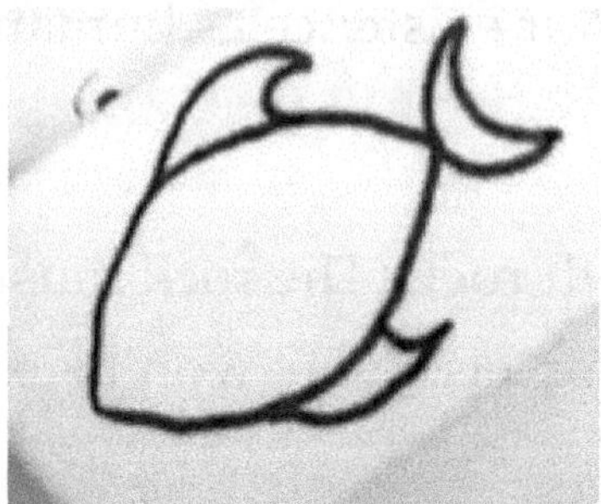

4. Then take up your color shift blue-violet flash paint to fill the fish on its tail, lips, fins, and body. When done, please leave it to dry on your rock.

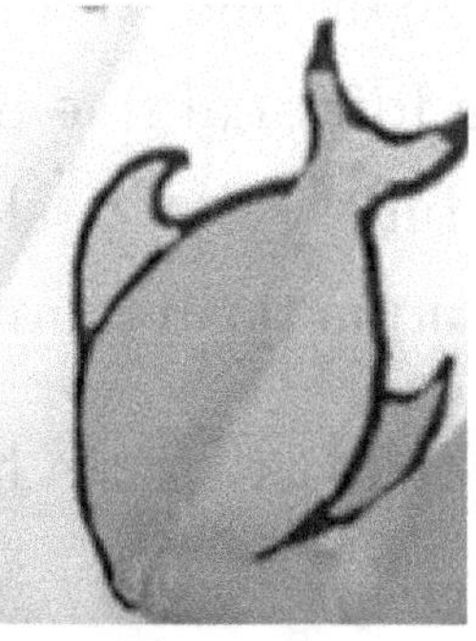

5. Get your stiff paintbrush and put any purple shade like Glitterific paint on your fish body.

6. Keep on applying the Glitterific paint until you like how your fish is glittering. Once done, simply leave it to dry. Under normal

circumstances, the glitterific paint will dry between a period of 13 hours to 14 hours.

7. Once it has dried, use your black posca pen to design your fish with its scales. You can also choose to add more design quality to your fishtail and fins.

8. Furthermore, include highlight dots to your fish's eye. This can be done when you add one small and one large white dot to its eye, respectively.

9. If you prefer to have bubbles on your fish rock, take up your white pen and add dots for bubbles on the place you want. If you like, you can also sketch the bubbles.

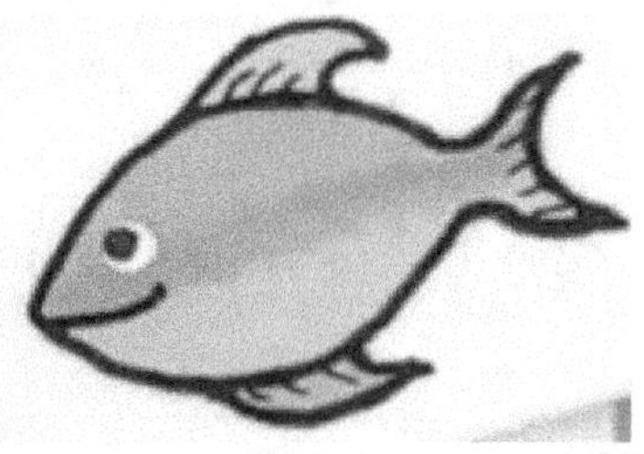

10. Once you have completed everything above, leave your rock to dry.

11. Lastly, seal your rock with 3 coats of spray sealer, and you have your fish painted rock ready for display.

Ladybug

Do you want to add extra beauty to your home garden? Well, the ladybug painted rock can certainly add more beauty to your household garden.

According to many, the ladybug brings good luck to homes, so you may just want to get this painted rock design in your home. This design is simple, and it is just about the perfect rock painting design for beginners to do.

Supplies

- Smooth rocks
- Pencil
- Mod Podge (This material is not compulsory to use)
- Posca pens

NOTE – One crucial tip to be aware of is that when you begin using new markers, ensure you forcefully shake your pens and experiment with them on a different rock before going on with this project. This will go a long way in revealing how the pens will work on your rock.

How to paint a ladybug on a rock

1. First of all, wash your chosen rock with warm water. Allow it to dry before you proceed with other steps. In most instances, it may take up to a day before your rock dries completely.

2. Once it has dried, paint your rock's body with a red pen. Then allow it to dry.

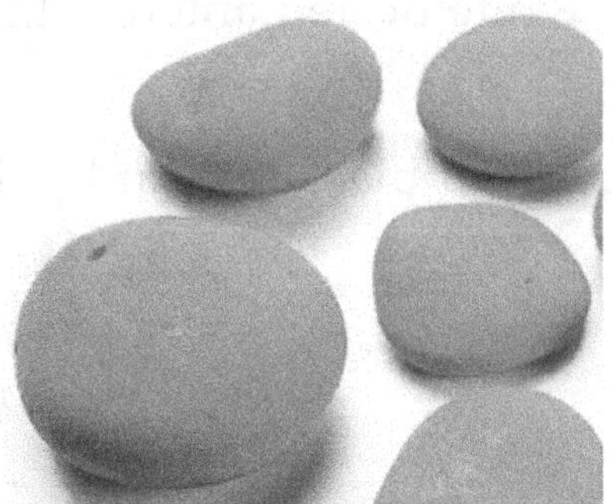

3. Proceed to paint the following after the red color has dried:
   - Blackhead
   - Vertical line
   - Black spots

As you have with the previous steps, also leave the paint to dry.

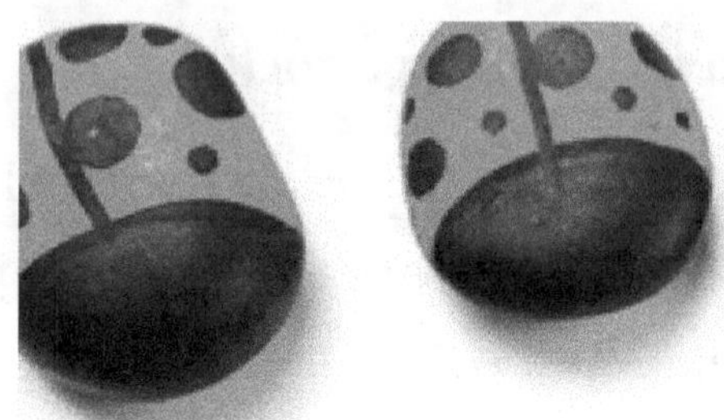

4. Apply white paint and create eyes on the blackhead.
5. Create white dotted antenna lines and leave them to dry.
6. Take up your black pen and paint its eyes.

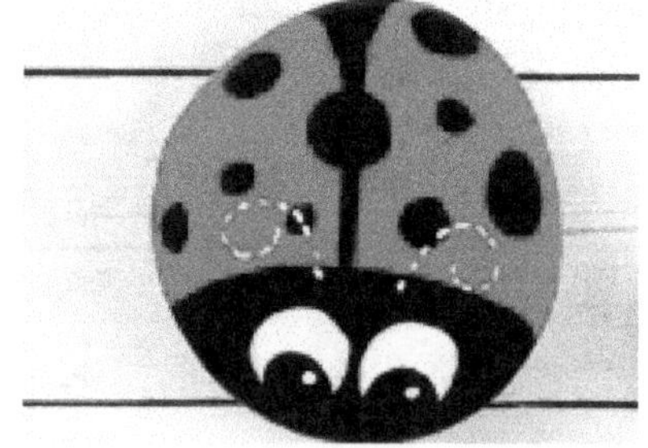

7. Conclude with painting the eyes by taking up your white market and painting a dot on the different eyes.

There you have it; you have painted a ladybug rock successfully. The beauty of using posca pens is that it takes only about 60 seconds to dry, leaving you with a faster process than earlier imagined.

Pumpkins

Pumpkins are used to celebrate Halloweens. Painted pumpkin rocks can be placed in the corner of your home. You can create many pumpkins rocks with your kid's help and get them to learn also.

Supplies

- Smooth rocks
- Clear spray sealer
- Posca paint pens (Orange, brown, and yellow, dark and light green colors)
- Paintbrush

How to paint pumpkin rocks

1. With your orange posca pen, sketch the shape of the pumpkin you want to draw. For a tip, you can

begin your sketch in the center, and it should look like the shape of a heart.

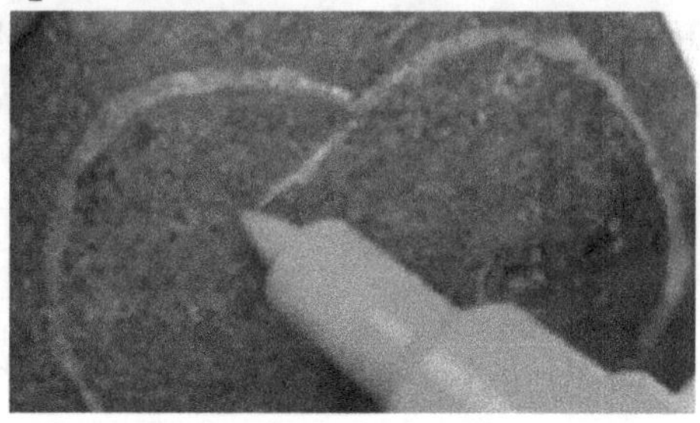

Another tip is that you should sketch two humps that emanate from the middle.

2. The next step in your process of painting pumpkin rocks is what is referred to as flooding. It works by placing your pen on the rock and pressing it as you release its contents.

Its contents will contain paint used with a paintbrush to distribute it to your sketched pumpkin shape.

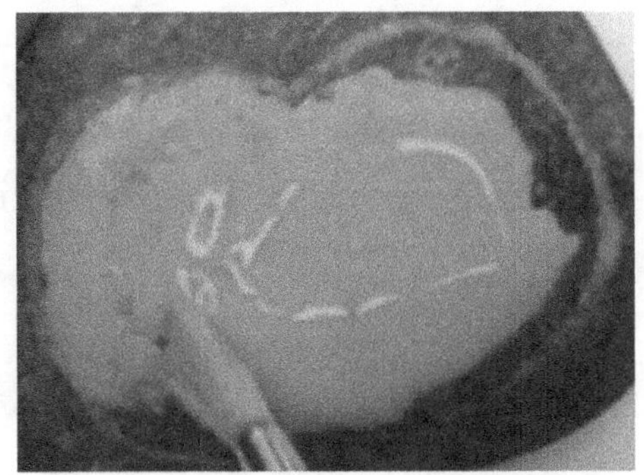

3. Take up your brown posca pen and sketch the orange pumpkin shape and include contour lines.

4. As you have with your brown posca pen, take up your yellow posca pen and include yellow highlight lines to provide your pumpkin with a different look.

5. Next, use the light green paint pen to sketch or draw a stem on the pumpkin rock. It is more advisable to draw a long stem that features a curly-cue on the top. Alternatively, you can choose to draw a short stem as well.

6. Add stem contours. The dark green posca marker is used to draw contour lines to the stem. You can also sketch the edges of your pumpkin stem.

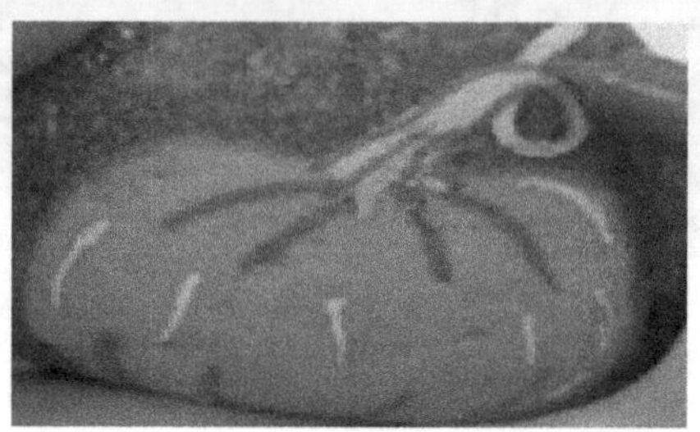

7. Seal the pumpkin rock. The last step is to use your clear spray sealer material to seal the pumpkin rock. Once done sealing the pumpkin rock, leave it to dry outdoors.

TIP – If you want to use your rock to play a game of hiding and seek, do well to tag the back of the pumpkin rock with a posca pen before you seal the rock.

Turtle

Do you want to get your kids so excited? Well, with a turtle paint rock, you can make them happy. Kids love the sight of beautifully painted rocks, and painting a rock with a turtle design can make them excited.

Now, what do we need to paint an attractive turtle on a rock? Look below for the materials needed to paint a turtle rock

Supplies

- A round or oval-shaped rock. In addition, you will also have to get 5 little oval-shaped rocks to serve as the turtle's legs and heads. While trying to find a round or oval-shaped rock, ensure they are flat.
- Brushes
- Different paint such as acrylic paint
- Seal varnish
- Glue gun. Alternatively, if your kids will be joining you in painting the turtle rocks, use a low temp glue gun instead.
- Black, green, and cream markers (The markers need to be permanent)

How to paint a turtle rock

1. Wash your rocks and allow them to dry under the sun.

2. Using your permanent green marker, go on to color your round or oval-shaped rock green.

3. Use your cream marker and color the largest rock. Then leave it to dry as well.

4. When the cream color has dried on your rock, use your marker to draw the turtle shell. A quick tip in this step is to use a pencil to sketch the turtle shell before drawing it. This will prevent you from making mistakes.

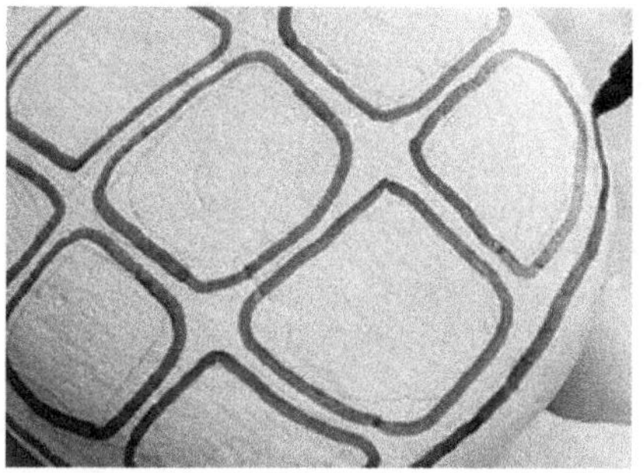

5. Color the turtle shells using the permanent green marker. Often, people use olive green to color the turtle shells.

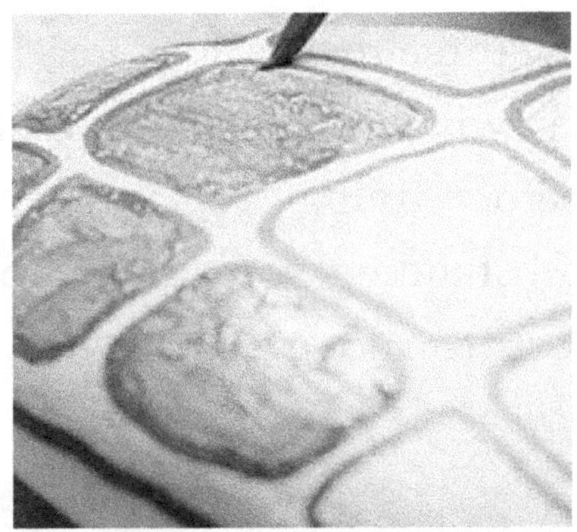

6. Leave the green color to dry. While waiting for your turtle rock to dry, you can produce heat to the glue gun.

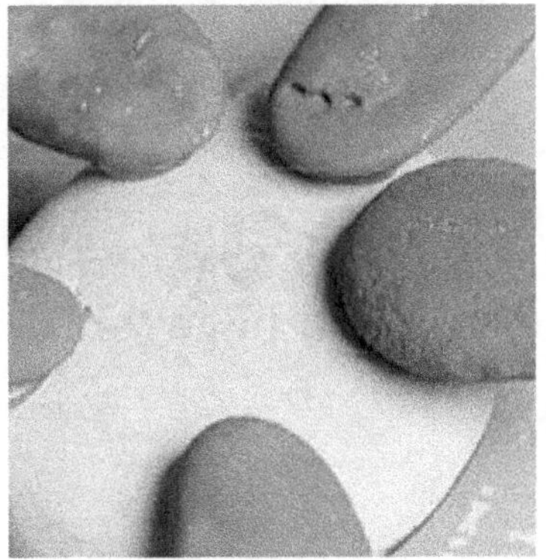

7. After heating the glue gun for some time, you can now glue the head and legs to the turtle shell's lower side. If you have the time to spare, it is much more advisable to use white school glue to

glue the three rocks. However, the only downside to using white school glue is that it will take some time before drying.

8. Notwithstanding your glue choice, simply draw the nostrils and eyes using a black permanent marker.

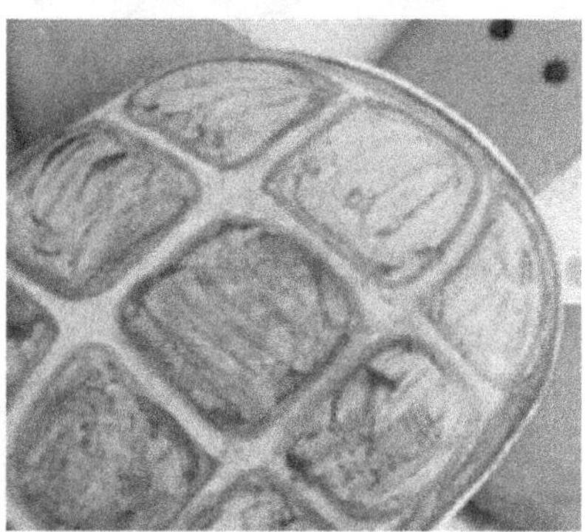

9. There you have it, allow the permanent marker to dry, and you will have your well-crafted painted turtle rock.

Country Flags

If you want to enter into the excitement of any sporting events like the Olympics, you will cherish the activity of designing and painting flag rocks.

Some major sporting events like the world cup or the summer Olympics is the perfect time to teach someone how to create painted flag rocks. They can even be placed in schools and homes to signify the country you love.

Flag rocks are painted depending on the country you choose to design. For example, you can decide to paint a rock with the United States of America flag design or a Brazilian design.

Supplies

- Round rocks
- Markers
- Acrylic paint
- Pencil

How to paint a flag rock

Now, the idea here is to be creative because you are the one to choose the kind of flag you want to paint on your rock. The simple steps include:

1. Washing your rock and leaving to dry completely.

2. At this point, you should have decided on the flag you want to paint. If you haven't, you can still have a chitchat with your friends, kids, or within yourself and choose the flag you want to paint.

3. After a decision has been made, simply outline or sketch the flag design on your rock with a pencil.

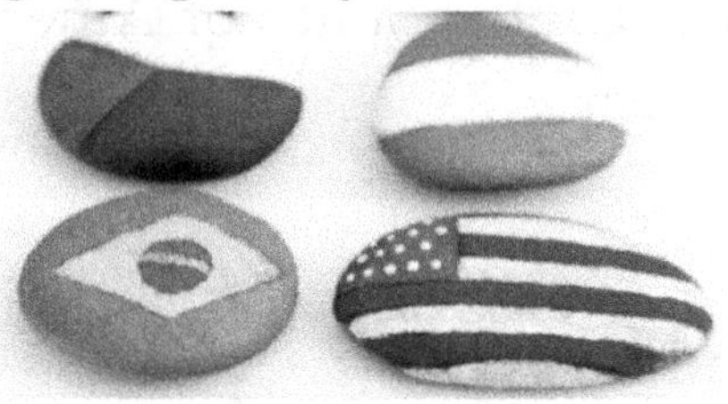

4. On the sketched rock, color the rock with your acrylic paint. On second thought, you can also use a marker to paint other sides of your rock if need be.

Zombie

Are you looking to scare your kids during the Halloween period? Well, you may just want to join your trick or treating exercise with some zombie painted rocks.

This process can be started and completed on the same Halloween day, so don't expect to waste time painting zombies on rocks.

Supplies

- Clear sealant spray
- Smooth rocks (Compulsory)
- Paint pens
- Paintbrush
- Green acrylic paint

How to paint zombie rocks

1. Use your green acrylic paint to coat your rock in 4 thin layers. Otherwise, you can also choose to use a green paint pen to coat your rock layers. If you used green acrylic paint, you would need to dry it before going to the next step.

2. Once dried, draw the zombie eyes with a white paint pen. This is recommended so that you won't stain the edge of the brush with other colors.

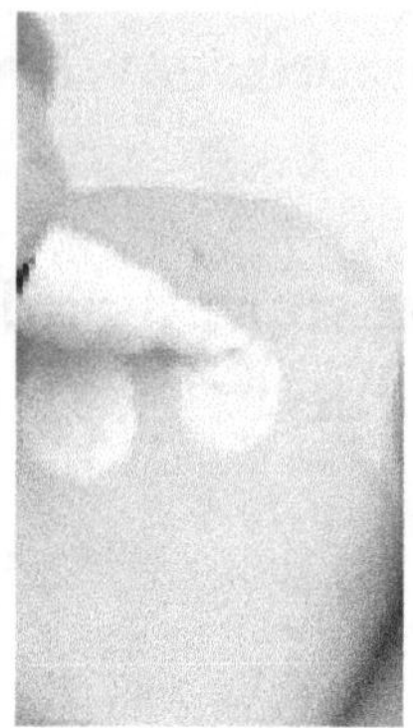

3. Also, draw the type of forehead or eye wrinkles you want with your green paint pen. Keep on drawing until you like the wrinkle that is present on your zombie rock.

4. Draw your zombie's nostrils holes and its mouth with your black paint pen. Allow it to dry before moving on.

5. With caution, create its teeth while using the already assembled white paint pen.

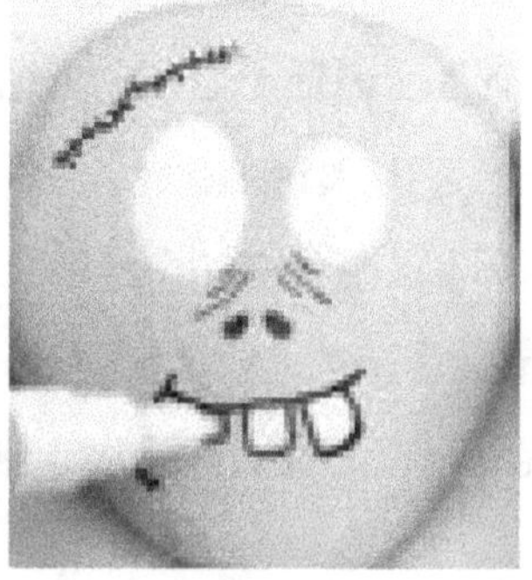

6. Sketch the eyes and draw the eye pupils with a black paint pen.

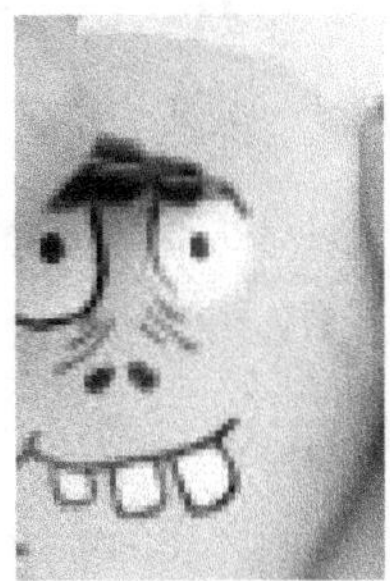

7. If you like, you can draw the zombie's brains with your pink paint pen.
8. Another elective choice you can make for your zombie rock is to seal it with a spray sealant. This step is usually advisable because it helps preserve your zombie rocks to last for a long time.

Strawberry

As a beginner, strawberry painted rocks are the perfect way to begin your rock painting journey. It is a creative drawing that can add to your portfolio of painted rocks.

It can be used to decorate your garden and even your kitchen. Look below as we reveal the supplies needed and steps to follow to paint strawberry rocks.

Supplies

- Rocks (small-sized rocks is perfect for painting strawberries)
- Paintbrushes (for this, you should get a single fine tip brush and another flat tip brush)
- Acrylic paint in different colors, including apple green, black tie, turf green, school bus, and lipstick
- Toothpick
- Wax paper

How to paint strawberry rocks

1. Wash your rocks to remove all dirt and dry them afterward.
2. Get a wax paper or a newspaper sheet and place them down to protect the top of your rock from getting stained.
3. Paint the whole rock surface in lipstick red with your flat tip paintbrush.
4. Allow the lipstick red color to dry on the surface of your rock.

5. Go through the same process for another coat to cover the entire rock. A quick piece of information about this process is that it is better to paint one side of your rock before moving to the next side. This will prevent the paint from sticking or gluing to your rock's surface.

6. Get your toothpick and dip a side of it into the black-tie acrylic paint color. Also, add a little vertical line across the red-painted rock.

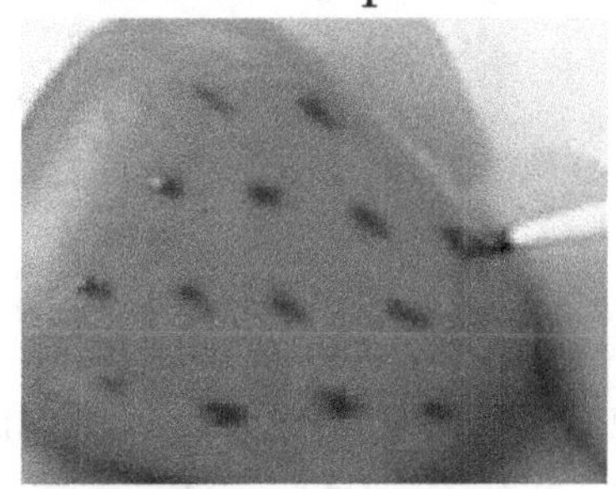

7. Keep on adding the edges of the toothpick into the paint in the middle of the dashes created. Be very careful because you still need to maintain similar dashes on the other side of your rock. Once done, allow the paints to dry.

8. Dip the toothpick into the school bus yellow acrylic paint color on the black dashes surface and allow it to dry.

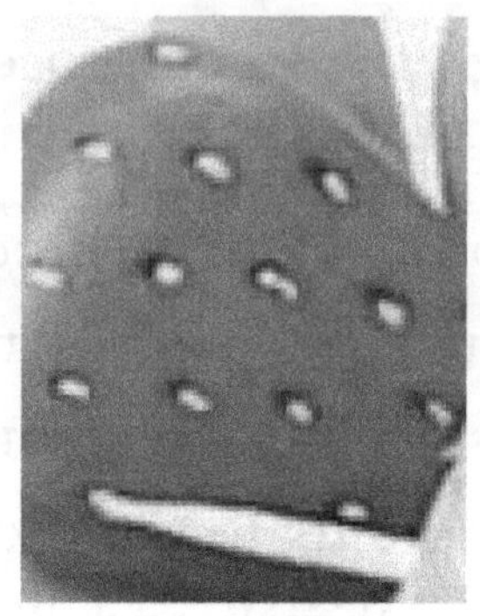

9. Get your fine tip paintbrush and put your brush into the apple green acrylic paint. From there, you can now paint the greenery to your strawberry rock.

    Paint one side before moving to the other sides to prevent the surface from sticking. Leave the paints to dry on the rock.

10. Last of all, put your fine paintbrush into the turf green color and go on to paint an extra green shade on the body of the apple green sides.

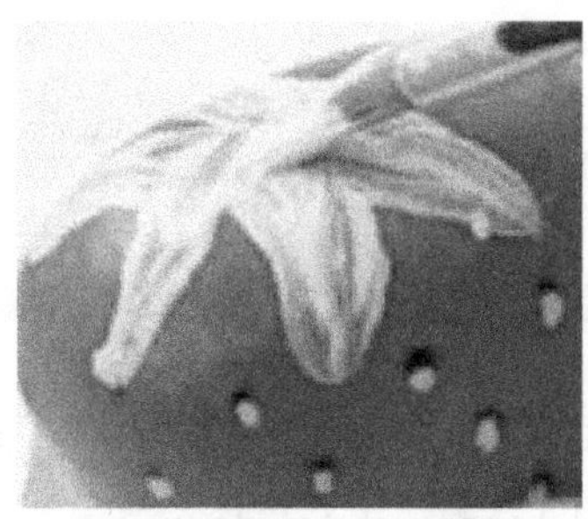

11. As with other steps, leave the green color paint to dry before displaying your painted strawberry rock.

Toy Story Alien

Are your kids free to learn something new? Why not teach them how to make toy story alien rocks? Of course, they will feel excited that they are about to make their favorite Disney movie characters.

If you are ready, so are we. So let's get right to it.

Supplies

- Smooth rocks (Compulsory)
- Clear spray sealant
- Paintbrushes
- White acrylic paint

- Pencil
- Paint pens

How to paint toy story alien rocks

1. Wash your rock to remove every dirt, sand, or filth, and leave it to dry.
2. If you want to use a dark rock, you will have to paint the rock with white acrylic paint on the 4 coats. Get a white-colored rock instead so as not to go through this stress.
3. Using a pencil, sketch, or draw out the toy story alien. A paint pen should follow the sketching.
4. If you want to draw the toy story's head, you need to start by creating a large shape that looks like a football. A light green paint pen should work just fine to sketch and color its head.

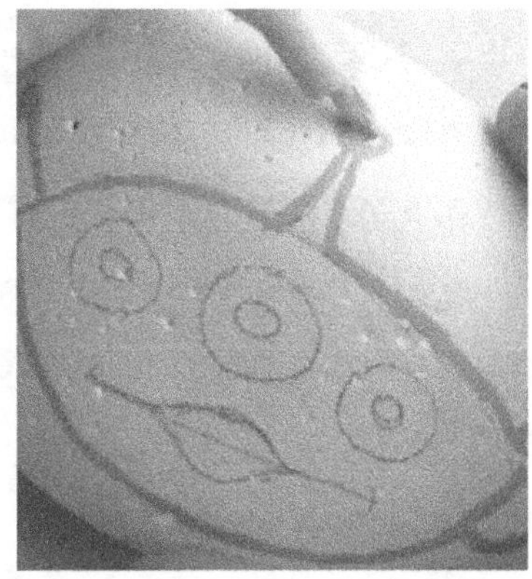

5. Sketch and draw the alien's antenna by creating a small and tall triangular shape on his head's center.

6. You can also draw a small-sized circle on its head and color the antenna with a light green paint pen.

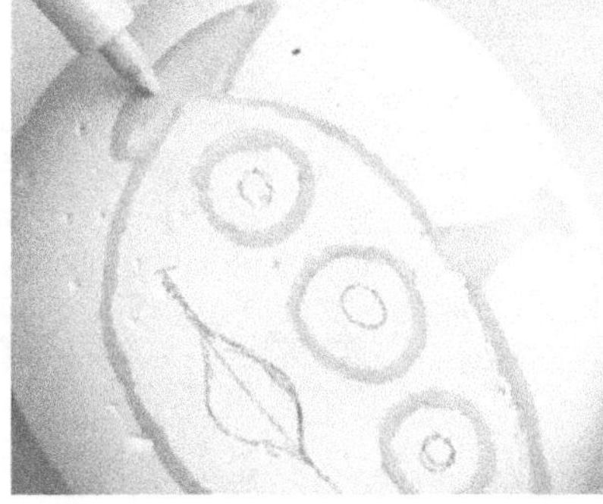

7. Now to the ears. Draw on the ears by sketching a long line in and outside from one side of the

head. Also, use the pencil to draw a triangular shape on the other side of the head. Afterward, color his ears with a light green paint pen.

8. Create the alien's eyes by drawing a large and circle eye in his head's center, underneath the antenna.

9. Then draw his eyeballs on both sides of the middle eye. Draw the two eyeballs a bit underneath the middle eye. For the inner eye, a black paint pen would work perfectly.

10. Depending on what you want, you can either choose to draw a smile or make its face simple. Use a black paint pen when drawing a smile on the alien's face.

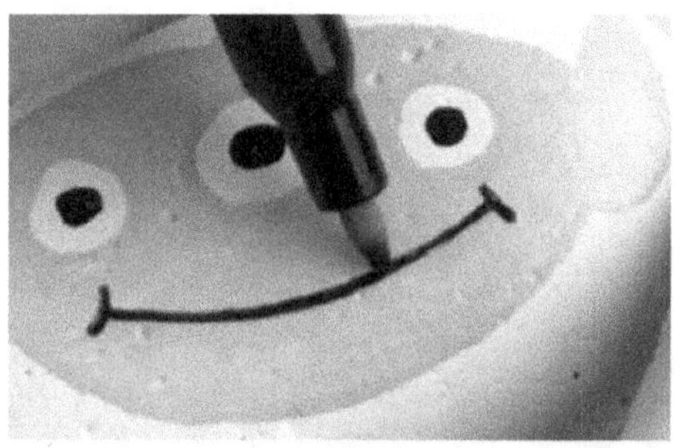

11. Optionally, you can use a sealant spray to preserve the painted toy story alien rocks for long periods.

12. Follow the same design process listed above for other rocks you want to paint.

Dot Mandala

If you want to make well-crafted dot mandala rocks, but you don't know how to? We have the right step by step guide to direct you on how to make one.

You don't need to have mastered the art of rock painting before painting mandala rocks. Also, dot mandala rock painting is a perfect opportunity for beginners to start their rock painting career. Most dot mandala rocks are sophisticated and beautiful.

Supplies

- Rocks
- Water-based acrylics paints (DecoArt is recommended)
- Dotting tools
- Brushes
- Toothpick or pin

How to paint dot mandala rocks

1. To begin painting, you need first to wash your rocks to remove the hidden dirt.
2. Locate the middle of the rock.
3. Create a small dot in the center of the rock by using a dotting tool.
4. Proceed and create an X with the use of small dots around the center dot.
5. In the last step, some people only use paint to paint the middle to form circles.
6. Divide the circles into half with different smaller dots.

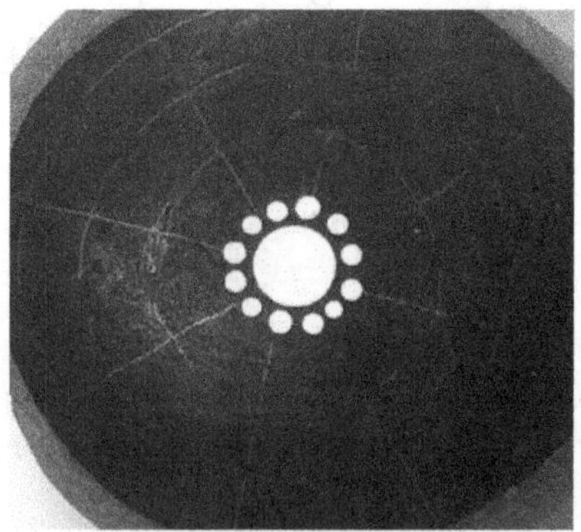

7. Take up a new paint color, include a single dot in the V of every small dots you made.

8. Keep on adding the superior dots in the V within your rock.

9. Once done, you can begin adding small dots. A quick tip here is to make your dotting tip small. This is where you either need a toothpick or a pin.

10. From the outside dot edge, position one dot and go through to the other side of your circle.

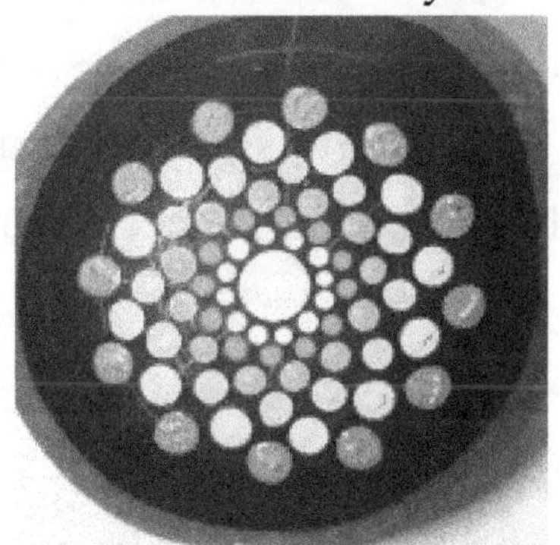

11. Your dotting tool should not have more paint on several dots. Ensure you do not rush this process so you don't make a mistake.

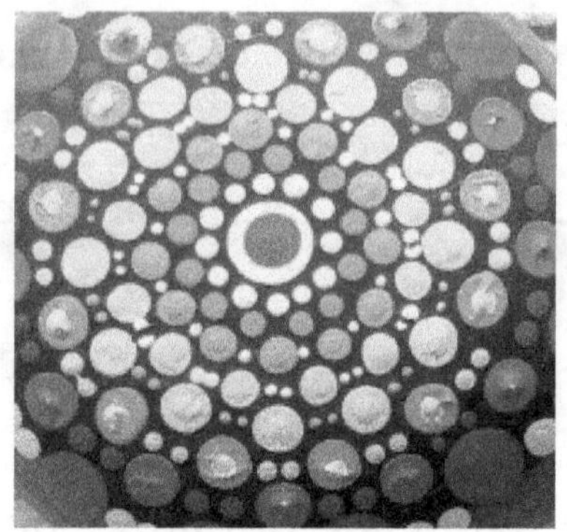

12. Don't forget to raise your tool high, so you don't fall guilty dragging the dots with you.

13. There you have it, you have created a dot mandala rock design successfully.

Rock Sharks

Are you going to the beach to have some fun? Why not paint some shark rocks while on your way? Indeed, it will interest people you will meet at the beach and others that will go with you.

The process is pretty straightforward, and it only requires some minutes to complete. It is also a good option for non-professionals to show their creative skills.

Supplies

- Some small paint brushes
- Medium triangular rock with a flat surface (It has to be a triangle, just like the shape of a real shark)
- Acrylic paints in lipstick read, dolphin gray, cotton ball white, and black time color (DecoArt Americana Multi-Surface paints are recommended)

How to paint rock sharks

1. Wash your rock and leave them to dry.
2. Then paint a triangular-shaped look-like nose with your Acrylic cotton ball white paint color.

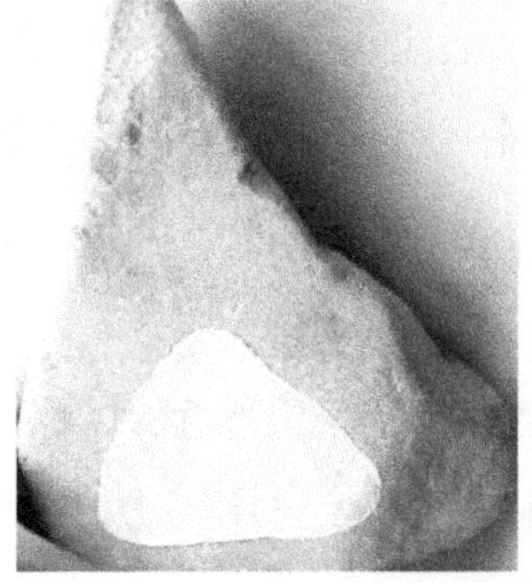

3. Leave the white color paint to dry before painting another coat.

4. Sketch the look-like nose and fill other sides of the rock with the dolphin gray acrylic paint.

5. Also, sketch the external rim of the white look-like nose with a small white and gray mixture.

6. Paint its two eyes at both sides of the head using black acrylic paint.

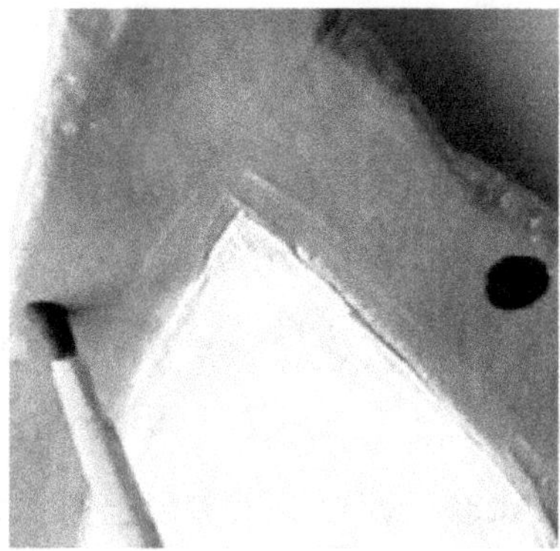

7. Join small quantities of white and black and draw crescents within the exterior side of the eyes.

8. Sketch and paint an oblong mouth with the red acrylic paint.

9. Outline the teeth with red paint and fill them. Leave it to dry for a while before painting another coat if need be.

10. Depending on the outcome, you can wipe the snout using a few extra white paints.

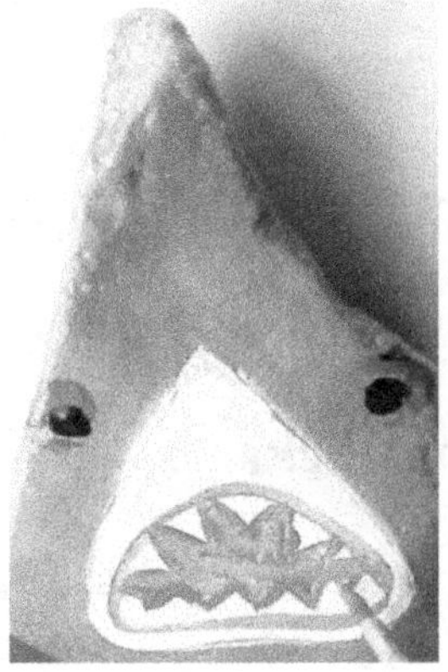

11. Once done, leave the painted rock shark to dry.

12. Now, you have your painted shark rock that you can take to the beach and play with.

Minion

For a beginner, the minion rock is something that cannot be exempted or over-looked. It is an easy rock painting design that does not require too many materials or additional time.

Minions are so loveable by kids and adults alike, and they are perfect for rock painting.

Supplies

- Rocks

- Paintbrushes
- Acrylic paint of blue, yellow, and white colors.
- Sharpies (Black ultra-fine tip, silver, and black fine tips are needed)

How to paint minion rocks

1. After gathering your rocks, wash them, and leave them to dry.
2. Paint your rocks with yellow color.
3. After the yellow has dried, use the blue acrylic paint and paint the underside.

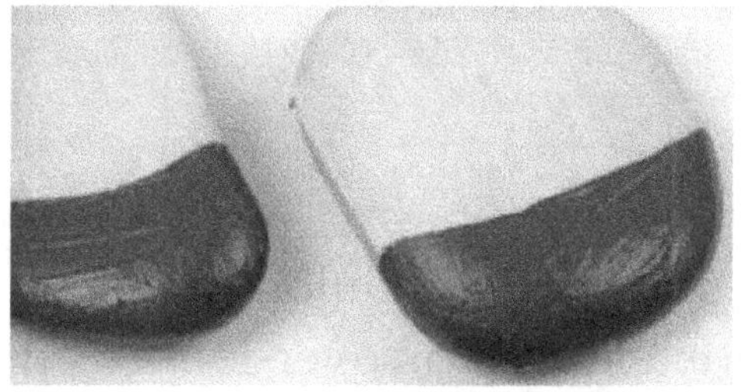

4. Draw the minions' two eyes with white paint. Leave the white paint to dry before using your sharpies.
5. Also draw the eyes using silver sharpies.

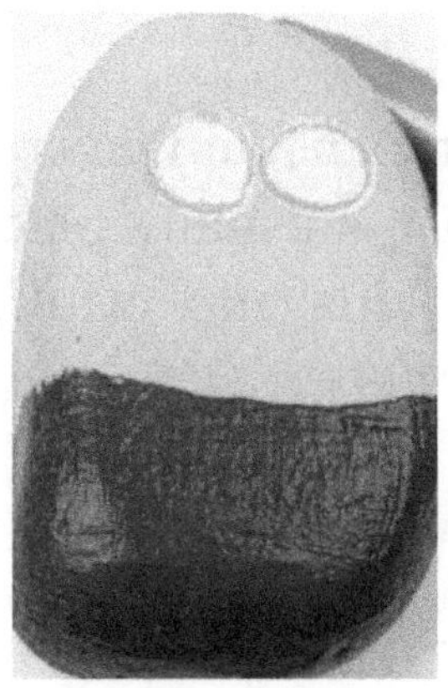

6. Mark the eyes, give the minions expressions, and Google strap using a fine black sharpie.

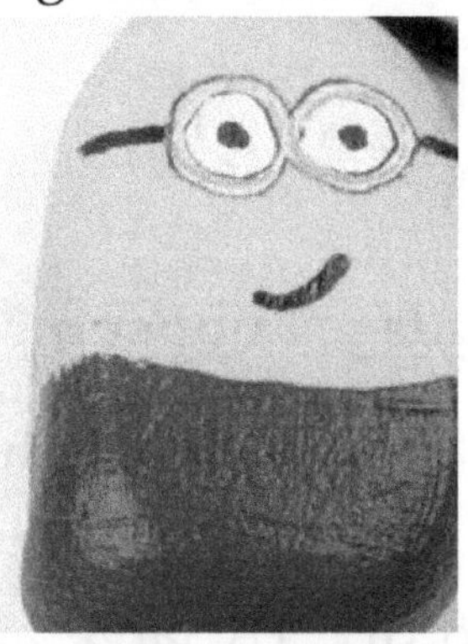

7. There you have it; you can display your minions indoors. However, if you want to move it outside your home, you should get a spray sealant.

Vintage Camper

The vintage camper painted rock is a colorful and beautiful rock that is usually placed indoors to decorate the home. Both kids and adults can paint a vintage camper rock.

Supplies

- Large rocks
- DecoArt Americana Paint (Snow white, light green, turquoise blue, lamp black, pink).
- Chalk
- Paintbrush
- Spray sealer

How to paint vintage camper rock

1. Start the process by washing your sizeable flat rock with water to remove the hidden stains and allow it to dry. (A large and flat rock is needed because painting is much easier on it).
2. With your chalk, decorate the vintage camper design on its body. The exciting thing here is that you don't have to be perfect while designing the rock's surface with chalk.

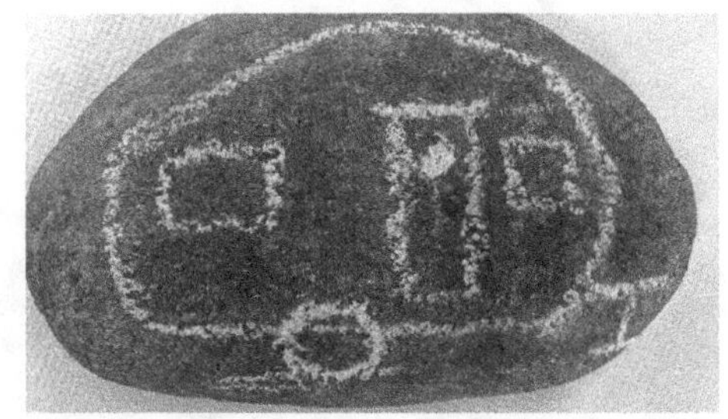

3. Take up a small and flat paintbrush and cover the vintage camper with colors. You can use turquoise blue on the lower half of the vintage camper, while a snow-white paint will serve the upper part.

4. Additionally, a grey sky color will work perfectly for the windows, and for the doors, you need to use a pink poodle skirt.

5. Ensure you allow the colors to dry completely before moving to the subsequent stages.

6. Proceed to sketch the camper in black paint with a fine tip paintbrush. Then add yellow color to the outlined curtains.

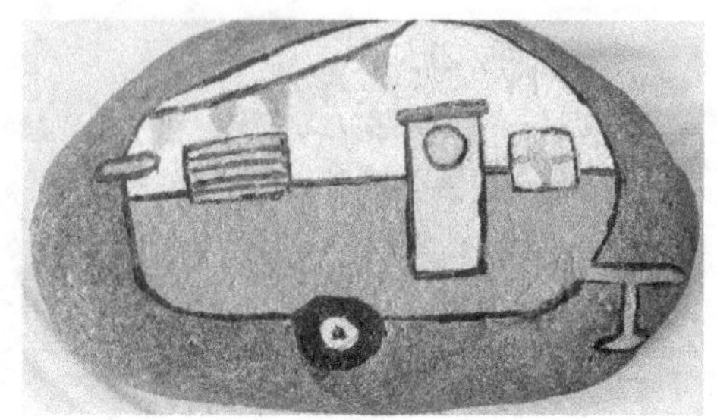

7. Leave it to dry before spraying the vintage camper rock with a spray sealer. This last step is optional, but it is fully recommended to display its design outside your home.

Candy Corn

The candy corn rock design is yet another paint design that serves well during the Halloween period. Beginners and intermediate rock artists can use this project to learn and improve on their creativity level.

If you are motivated by the candy corn rock's looks, why not make a move and create one for yourself or others. Meanwhile, here are the supplies needed to paint one:

Supplies

- Triangular rock

- Acrylic paint (Yellow, Black, Orange, and White)
- Large paintbrushes
- Spray sealer
- Detailed paintbrushes

How to paint candy corn rocks

1. Wash your rock and dry it.
2. Paint every nook and cranny of the triangular rock with orange acrylic paint and leave to dry.
3. Paint the longer side of the triangular rock with yellow acrylic paint.

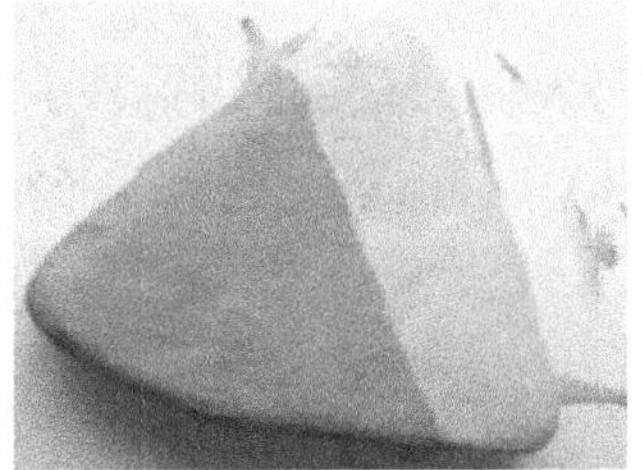

4. Then paint the top tip of the triangular rock with white acrylic paint. Also, leave it to dry.
5. You could either choose to leave it this way or continue painting. If you choose to continue, you can use the detail paintbrush and draw the eyes.

The eyes should be drawn between the orange and yellow sides.

6. Paint a small mouth just beneath the eyes and create white dots in the candy corn eyes. (4 white dots should do just fine for the eyes).

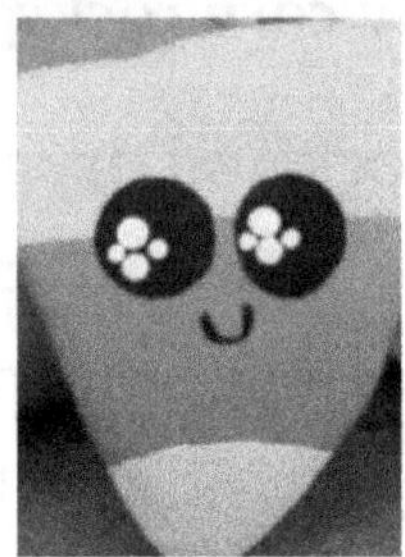

7. Spray the candy corn rock with a coat sealer to prevent it from damaging, especially if used for outdoor purposes.

Watermelon

The watermelon rocks are a great way to start your rock painting journey. Since the fruit itself is attractive, you may just want to design a rock that looks exactly like it.

Once painted, it can be used to decorate your kitchen or any other part of your home.

Supplies

- Rocks (River rocks works best)
- Mod Podge
- Acrylic paint (Pink and Red)
- Paintbrushes
- Paint pens (2 shades of black, white, and green)
- Paint palette

How to paint watermelon rocks

1. Purchase or find your river rocks and prepare them the right way.
2. Clean your rocks with water and soap and allow them to dry.
3. Paint your rock's base coat when you rock finally dries.
4. To produce the watermelon shade, you are expected to mix pink and red acrylic paint colors in the paint palette.
5. In some instances, you may have to paint multiple coats, but this is dependent on the paint and rock color you are using.

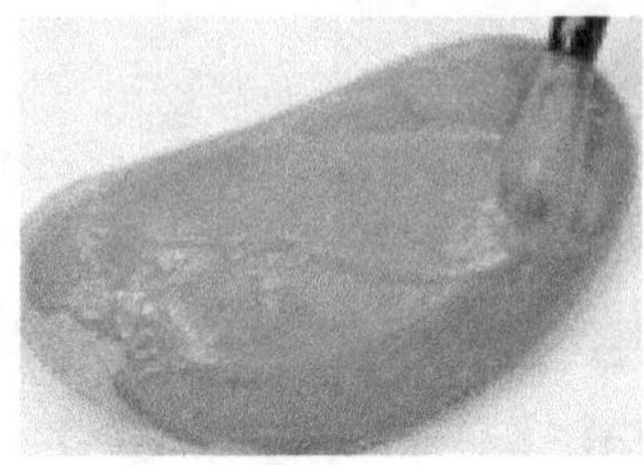

6. If you are painting 2 coats or more, ensure you allow the first coat to dry before moving over to the second coat.
7. Paint two different shades with your green color using your paint pens. For example, you can use fine tip paint pens.
8. You can begin with the much darker green shade before the thinner green light color.
9. If you want, you can add a face to your watermelon rock. A black and white fine tip paint pen can be used to outline eyes.

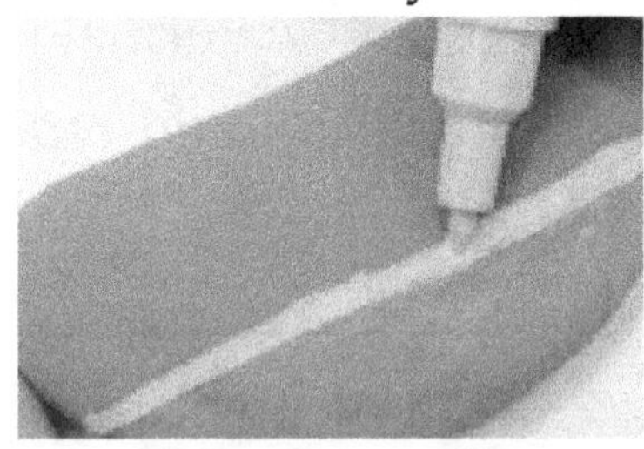

10. Outline the watermelon seeds using a black paint pen.

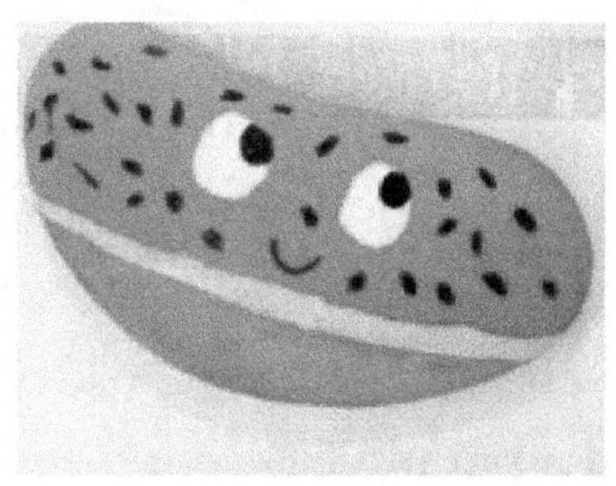

11. Lastly, you need to seal your painted watermelon rock with a spray sealer or Mod Podge.

Sugar Skulls

Sugar skulls are created for celebrating scary events, and they are easy designs for beginners. Within 15 minutes, you can paint a sugar skull rock successfully.

Supplies

- Oval shaped rock
- Paint pen
- Acrylic paints

How to paint sugar skull rocks

1. Wash your oval-shaped rock thoroughly and allow it to dry.
2. Cover your rock with a coat of lightened up colored paint and wait till it dries.
3. Next, you should add an extra coat of similar color paint and allow it to dry. If you want, you can add a paint coat.
4. Outline the nose, mouth shapes, and eyes on the rock (this can be done with a black paint pen).

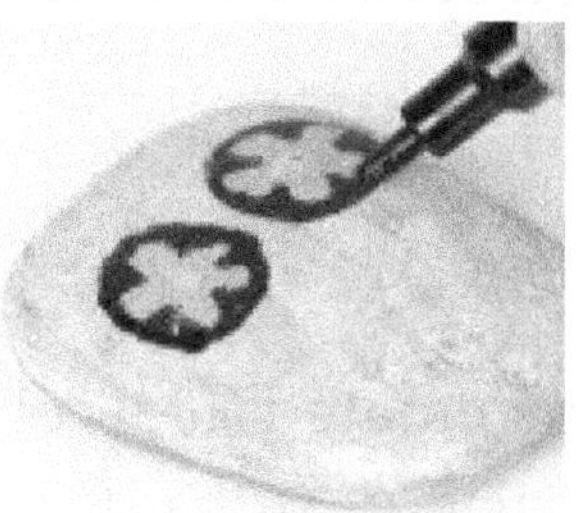

5. Using other colorful and beautiful paint colors, draw the skill with dots, flowers, or other attractive shapes.

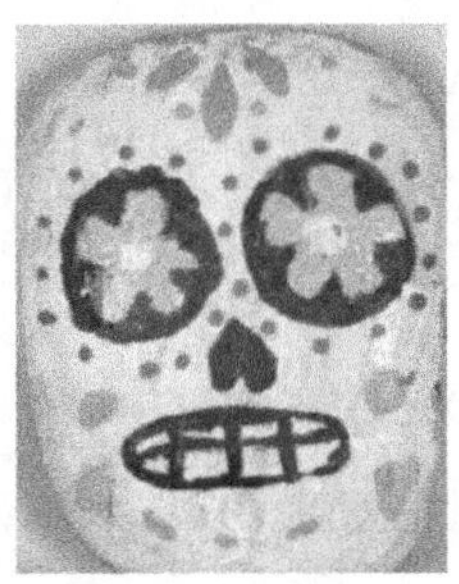

Bunny Rocks

Another fun rock painting design is the charming bunny rocks. Kids often love them, so if you want to get your kids all excited, you can paint a bunny rock for them.

Supplies

- Rock
- Small paintbrush
- Sealant (optional)
- White acrylic paint
- Paint pens

How to paint bunny rocks

1. As you have with other rock painting designs, you also have to wash your rocks and leave them to dry.

2. Use your paint to decorate one side with light green and the other side with light blue.

3. Leave the base to dry before using a white paint pen to draw a small circle, which will serve as the head. For the body, draw a large circle.

4. To sketch the ears, draw a thin, tall triangle.

5. Paint the top of your created small circle with a white paint pen.

6. The aim of painting a bunny on the rock is to make it light gray. This means you only have to paint the rock with little black paint.

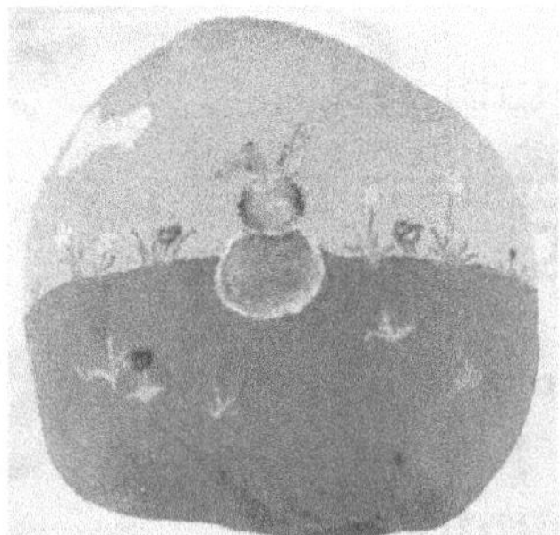

7. Next, use a little amount of white acrylic paint and paint the base coat.

8. The green paint pens should be used to paint the grass sides beside the horizon line (This is where the Easter eggs and flowers will be added).

9. Keep on painting with your black and white paint pen on the bunny base.

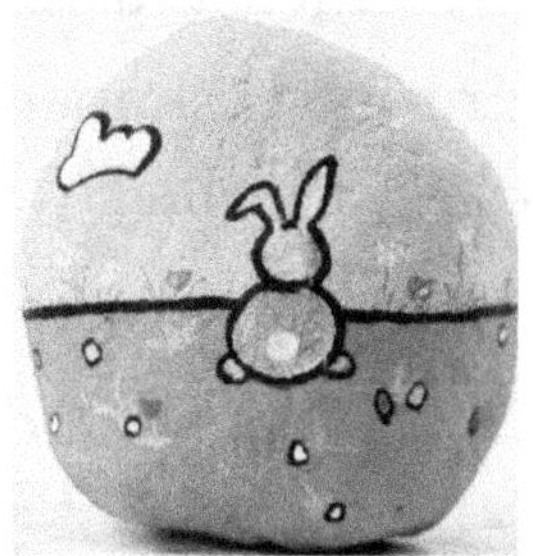

Easter Egg

Ready to get your Easter celebration all kicked-off? Well, an Easter egg rock can perfectly make your celebration worthwhile. When prepared to paint your Easter egg rock, you can rally your kids with you and teach them the easy procedures.

Supplies

- Rocks (It should be an oval-shaped rock)
- Paint palette
- Waterproof sealers

- Small and medium paintbrushes
- Q-tips
- Acrylic paint (pastel colors)

How to paint Easter egg rocks

1. Clean your rock water and soap and leave to dry. Make sure your rock is shaped in egg form.
2. Prepare your paint colors and paint your rock coat. You can paint one or two coats, depending on the paint color you selected.

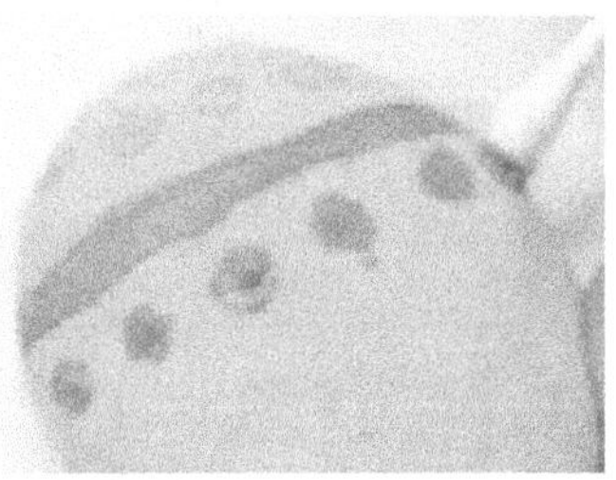

3. Ensure your paint coats are on the thinner rock part.
4. Take up your small paintbrushes and design lines, squiggles, and zigzags using any color.
5. Also, create dots using your Q-tips.

6. Once the paints have dried successfully, you can now seal it with a waterproof sealer to use the rocks outside.

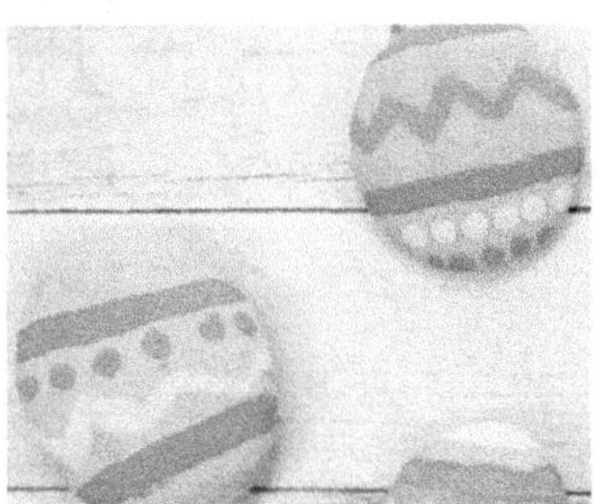

Snake

Snake rocks are one of the few rock painting designs that require more than one rock. It is also a colorful pattern design that is fun to make.

Supplies

- Up to 12 smooth and black rocks (we recommend you purchase them from a craft store)
- Red felt
- Paint markers
- Hot glue gun
- Googly eyes

How to paint snake rocks

1. Place the 12 flat and black rocks in your art room.
2. Use the paint markers to outline patterns on 11 of your 12 rocks. Depending on what you deem fit, you can choose to create 2 different pattern types on your rock. Leave the paint to dry on your rock.
3. Take up your red felt and cut a snake tongue. Then get your hot glue gun and attach it to the last rock.
4. Attach two googly eyes to the head of your snake.
5. Place all the rocks once more and carefully arrange them to make a perfect snake art.

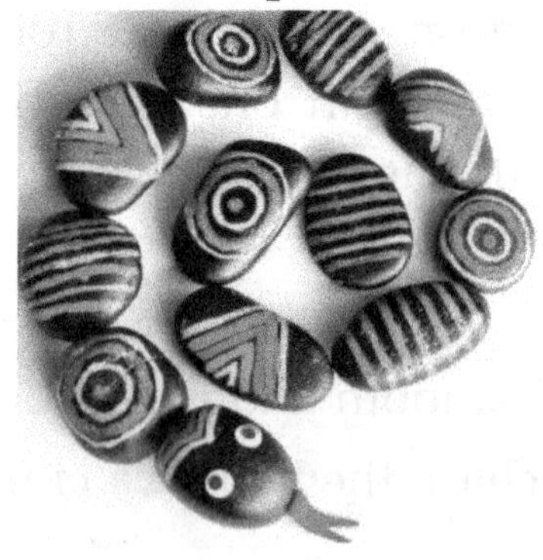

The end... almost!

Hey! We've made it to the final chapter of this book, and I hope you've enjoyed it so far.

If you have not done so yet, I would be incredibly thankful if you could take just a minute to leave a quick review on Amazon

Reviews are not easy to come by, and as an independent author with a little marketing budget, I rely on you, my readers, to leave a short review on Amazon.

Even if it is just a sentence or two!

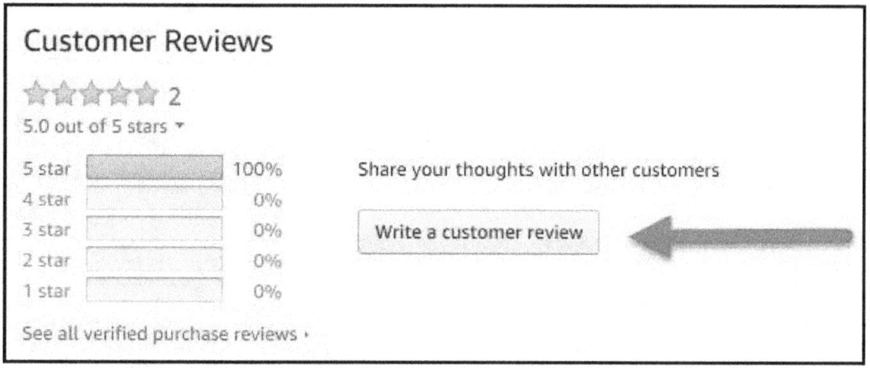

So if you really enjoyed this book, please...

>> Click here to leave a brief review on Amazon.

I truly appreciate your effort to leave your review, as it truly makes a huge difference.

Chapter 6

Rock Painting Frequently Asked Questions (Q&A)

Are you a rock painter, or you are looking to become one? If that is the case, we have compiled some essential rock painting frequently asked questions to assist you as you paint.

Rock painting is a fun activity perfect for both kids and adults. The frequently asked questions gathered in this section are questions asked by rock painting artists and those who seek to learn how to paint rocks.

If you are ready to go, so are we. Let's go!

Q – What is the best paint for rock painting?

Ans – The most recommended and advisable paint to use on rocks is Acrylics. It is also the most popular paint used by most experienced and beginner rock paint artists.

Acrylic paints are water-based, and they dry very quickly. You can get the paint from virtually every craft or art store. Other well-to-do brands for rock painting include:

- DecoArt
- Apple Barrel
- FolkArt

Additionally, acrylic paints also have a different range of paint options to choose from. For beginners who don't want to get into the hassle of mixing colors, they are advised to use craft paint.

Meanwhile, acrylic paint is not the only paint you can use on rocks; the likes of oil pastels, alcohol inks, watercolor paints, and chalk are also other good paint options. However, these selections are based on the rock painting design you want to do and the type of rock.

In summary, paints for rock paintings are numerous, but the most recommended and common is the acrylic paint.

Q – Is it essential to apply a base coat

Ans – No. It is not necessary to apply a base coat. However, applying a white base coat on gray rocks can make the color used on the rock brighten up, but this will need some paint coats.

Furthermore, while applying alcohol inks to paint rocks, a white base coat is important. It is vital. After all, it helps you to seal your rock because it is an absorbent material.

Alcohol inks are supposed to be applied on non-absorbent surfaces; this is why sealing rocks with a base coat is essential to give a non-absorbent surface area to paint easily.

Q – How do I trace an image on a rock if I am not experienced?

Ans – As a beginner, the best way to trace an image on a rock you want to paint is to do so with graphite paper.

Q – How long before I seal my painted rocks?

Ans – After painting your rock with any design, you should wait for at least 24 hours before sealing your painted rock. In a similar vein, it is recommended you wait for 2 days before sealing your paint-pouring rocks.

Some painted rocks can be sealed before 24 hours, but you cannot take any negative chance. Sealing of painted rocks is also dependent on the type of paint, the rock, and the number of paint layers.

If the paint does not dry fast, then 24 hours should be your minimum time before sealing your rock. Also, if the rock is a hard and rough one, you may have to wait until 24 hours before sealing your rock.

Q – Why should I seal my rocks?

Ans – Sealing rocks is the best way to preserve them for a long time. Furthermore, sealing rocks is also vital to protect them from different substances like moisture that can cause damages to them.

Spray sealers or any other sealer can help prevent your painted rock from nicks and scratches. Unless you want to keep your painted rocks indoors, you should always look for a reliable sealer and seal your rocks.

Q – What type of paint should I continue to use for dot painting?

Ans – The best paint type you should consistently use for a dot painting is acrylic paint. Acrylic paint is a unique paint type that contains thick contents like yogurt.

As a matter of fact, your painted rock may not be so exceptional if the paint you used is thin.

Q – How can I remove dried paint from the paintbrush?

Ans – After painting your rock, it is a bit frustrating to discover that some contents of the paint you used have dried on your paintbrush. However, don't bother so much because there is a solution to removing dried paint from the paintbrush.

Here's what you have to do to remove dried paint from your paintbrush:

- Pour 2tbsp of hand sanitizer gel into a cup.
- Spin your paintbrush in it for the dried paint to melt and remove.
- Once done, you can remove the paint from the paintbrush bristles.
- Lastly, rinse your paintbrush.

Q – How can I make a rock smooth to paint on?

Ans – Perhaps you just found a rock in your backyard, and you want to use it for your rock painting exercise, but you don't like the way it is looking. Well, you can always make a rough rock smoother before you start painting.

Any wood filler will make your rough rock smooth. Once the filler has dried, use light grit sandpaper to sand the rock surface before applying acrylic paint. The quantity of acrylic paint to be applied must only be a base coat.

Q – What is the rock painting materials needed to begin?

Ans – You don't have to spend a lot of money to purchase rock painting materials because they are not much. Rock painting exercise only needs a few materials.

The essential materials needed to start your rock painting journey are only rocks, paints, and paintbrushes. Meanwhile, there are other secondary materials needed to make your painted rock look attractive.

Some of the secondary materials needed to start painting rocks include:

- Paint pens
- Paint markers
- Dotting tools
- Sealers

Q – Brush-on or Spray? Which should I choose?

Ans – Choosing either a brush-on or spray rock sealer is dependent on what you like. Some people prefer to use a clear spray sealer because it is cheap and it is perfect for sealing many painted rocks at the same time.

Meanwhile, when selecting a rock sealer, ensure you select the one that provides UV protection to protect your rock and the one that resists outdoor moistures.

Q – How do I spray my painted rock?

Ans – It is recommended that you spray your painted rocks outside your home and not indoors. Alternatively, you can also spray your painted rocks in an open space.

The spray sealer produces strong and unpleasant odors that are harmful to human health. Another tip to follow while spraying your painted rocks is to give a minimum of 12 inches of space so that you won't get in contact with its content.

Start spraying your painted rock with a light coat before slowly adding more coats. After spraying your painted rock, wait for at least 24 hours before touching your rocks.

On the other hand, brush-on sealers are mostly used for painted rocks that are not situated outside the home.

Q – What is the best glue to join two or more rocks together?

Ans – One of the leading glues to attach two or more rocks is GE II Silicone Sealant. The GE II Silicone Sealant is an outdoor glue that is usually used to join two or more rocks for painting, and it is very efficient.

Other inefficient glues might only attach your rocks for some minutes, and you will discover they are miles apart after some time. Different glues serve their different functions. This means that a heavy rock will need a special type of glue, while light or smooth rock has its glue type.

Q – How large should my rock be?

Ans – Rock sizes are different, and they serve different paint designs. Depending on the painting design you want to make, you can either choose a large or small rock.

For example, to paint a shark rock, you need a large triangle-shaped rock, while to paint a dot mandala rock, you will need a small and smooth rock.

Q – What can I use to write an inspirational or educative message on rocks?

Ans – A paint pen or paint marker is what you should use to write an educative or inspirational quote on painted rocks. Don't try to use paint to write a message on a rock because it won't work.

Q – Can my kids join me in painting rocks?

Ans – Yes. Rock painting is perfect for both kids and adults. Your kids may even find the exercise interesting and will even like to paint for long periods.

Q – As a beginner, how long will it take to become a professional?

Ans – If you are just starting and you are painting rocks consistently, it should not take long before you become a professional.

While you may make mistakes initially, you can later consider yourself a professional if you make little or no mistakes when painting rocks.

Q – Can I make money from painting rocks?

Ans – Yes. Selling your rock painting designs can fetch you some money. People are willing to pay big money for painted rock designs that are beautiful and attractive.

You only have to look for the right place to sell your rock painting designs and get money in return.

Q – Can I send important messages with painted rocks?

Ans – Yes. You can use paint pens or paint markers and write important messages like inspirational quotes or informational quotes and show people around you.

Conclusion

As you can see, the process of painting rocks is easy and can be done by anyone. You don't need to be a professional before you can paint rocks. Although mistakes are bound to happen when starting, they are only there to shape you into becoming a rock painting expert.

Rock painting is an inexpensive art that, when completed, can fetch you some money. Painted rocks can also serve and share important peace messages to hostile communities.

Furthermore, this guide contains 20 different rock painting design ideas that are perfect for beginners.

If you are still confused about starting your rock painting journey, you should go through this guide once more.

Happy rock painting, artists !!!